MOUNTAIN BIKING

OUTDOOR PURSUITS SERIES

Don Davis
Dave Carter

Human Kinetics Publishers

Library of Congress Cataloging-in-Publication Data

Davis, Don, 1951-
   Mountain biking / Don Davis, Dave Carter.
     p.   cm. -- (Outdoor pursuits series)
   Includes bibliographical references (p.) and index.
   ISBN 0-87322-452-3
     1. All terrain cycling. I. Carter, Dave, 1946-   II. Title.
   III. Series.
   GV1056.D38   1993
   796.6'4--dc20   93-24692
                                       CIP

ISBN: 0-87322-452-3

Acquisitions Editor: Brian Holding; **Series Editor:** Holly Gilly; **Photo Editor:** Valerie Hall; **Assistant Editors:** Lisa Sotirelis and Dawn Roselund; **Copyeditor:** Stefani Day; **Proofreader:** Dawn Barker; **Production Director:** Ernie Noa; **Typesetter:** Sandra Meier; **Text Design:** Keith Blomberg; **Text Layout:** Denise Lowry and Tara Welsch; **Cover Photo:** Mark Thayer, Bell Sports; **Cover Design:** Jack Davis; **Interior Art:** Thomas • Bradley Illustration & Design; **Interior Photos:** credits on p. 140; **Models:** Marni Basic and Rick Bell; **Author Photos:** Bob Lickter (Dave Carter) and Alan Hardy (Don Davis); **Printer:** Bang Printing

Human Kinetics books are available at special discounts for bulk purchase. Special editions or book excerpts can also be created to specification. For details, contact the Special Sales Manager at Human Kinetics.

Printed in the United States of America   10 9 8 7 6 5 4 3 2 1

Human Kinetics Publishers
Box 5076, Champaign, IL 61825-5076
1-800-747-4457

Canada: Human Kinetics Publishers, Box 24040, Windsor, ON N8Y 4Y9
1-800-465-7301 (in Canada only)

Europe: Human Kinetics Publishers (Europe) Ltd., P.O. Box IW14,
Leeds LS16 6TR, England
0532-781708

Australia: Human Kinetics Publishers, P.O. Box 80, Kingswood 5062, South Australia
618-374-0433

New Zealand: Human Kinetics Publishers, P.O. Box 105-231, Auckland 1
(09) 309-2259

CONTENTS

1

GOING MOUNTAIN BIKING

Welcome to the adventure—the exciting, healthy, and rapidly growing world of mountain biking. Around the globe, popularity of the all-terrain bicycle (ATB) is on the climb. In fact, mountain biking is one of the world's fastest-growing outdoor activities. New riders of all ages are discovering the opportunities offered by the mountain bike. You can escape the risks of riding on busy streets and highways and see life from beyond the bicycle lane.

Mountain bikes are designed and built to be ridden off-pavement, on all kinds of terrain. Today's advanced models have a wide selection of gears to make climbing and descending hills much easier than it was on old-fashioned bikes. Shock absorption features and knobby tires smooth bumpy trails, add traction, and promote safety.

Escaping into nature aboard a mountain bike brings out the child in all of us. Age and fitness are not barriers; this is an activity each person can pursue at her or his own level. Cycling is easy on the body and great for all major muscle groups. And for stress reduction there is simply no better outlet.

The lure of mountain biking lies in its timeless, go-anywhere nature—the exploration of unknown trails and peaceful country backroads. From urban parks to alpine peaks, you can ride a mountain bike. It doesn't matter where you live.

Mountain biking will open new avenues of outdoor enjoyment and fitness for you. It comes as no surprise that joggers and walkers by the thousands are buying mountain bikes. For many people, pumping the pedals and covering 10 times the territory is an attractive alternative to pounding the pavement on foot. Gracefully you glide over hill and dale, enjoying the countryside with family and friends or building up sweat and your endurance level with a workout buddy. For combining exercise with fun and outdoor adventure, mountain bike riding is hard to beat.

If you've ridden any bike, you can ride a mountain bike. If you've never ridden before, the mountain bike is a great place to begin. The basic skills are minimal—you'll need a little practice with balance and on using the correct hands for braking and shifting gears. Of course, you'll need to think about bicycle safety as you get rolling. More advanced techniques will come later.

Now wobble down a bumpy dirt road and feel the interaction of your body with your bike. Sense just the right distribution of weight as you come around a turn and downshift in preparation for the hill ahead. Feel the wind in your face. It's just you, your bike, and the lay of the land.

Larry Pierce/F-Stock

Enjoying the spectacular vistas of Steamboat Springs, Colorado.

The Mountain Bike Difference

The mountain bike is perhaps the most efficient all-terrain vehicle under human power. It is easier to ride than its on-pavement counterpart, the road bike.

The mountain bike solves many of the problems that have turned some people away from bicycling. Among the advantages are the stability and cushioned ride provided by fat tires; wider gear selection with easy-access lever, button, or grip shifters; better brakes; and more comfortable body positioning.

Because of its rugged construction, the mountain bike generally needs less maintenance than road bikes. Of course, this doesn't mean you won't need to visit your bike shop for periodic tune-ups. It does mean fewer flat tires (despite use in tough terrain), as well as fewer wheel repairs and other problems associated with the more delicate road bikes.

Take a ride and see for yourself. You'll find a whole new feeling on a mountain bike.

What Is a Mountain Bike?

A mountain bike is built to be tough. It is designed for strength and durability, to take the hard knocks and rocks of off-road riding. Mountain bikes can be great on pavement, too, and that's where many cyclists spend most of their riding time. With a mountain bike, the cyclist really can enjoy the best of both worlds.

Mountain bikes normally have 15 to 24 speeds, which are controlled by derailleurs on the chainrings between the pedals and at the rear axle. Gears are controlled by top-mounted thumb shifters, rapid-fire under-the-grip button shifters, or grip shifters (like a motorcycle throttle) on the handlebar. Cantilever hand brakes provide ample stopping power.

One of the first differences you will notice about the mountain bike is the flat handlebar. It allows a comfortable upright, yet powerful, riding position. You may notice shock absorbers and fat, knobby tires for cushioned off-road traction. You'll see various water bottles, pumps, racks, bags, cycling computers, and other conveniences. More on those later.

Mountain bikes come in various sizes for youths and adults. Miniature mountain bikes are replacing the popular BMX bikes for many younger riders, especially those who ride with mom and dad. Some women's models are made, although many women choose men's bikes, which usually offer more options and are easier to carry and transport.

Types of Bicycles

Mountain Bike

Flat handlebars, fat and knobby tires, cushioned seat, shock absorbers (optional), 15 to 24 speeds. Lever, button, or grip shifting. Powerful hand brakes. Solid, stable ride. Strong and lightweight frame materials.

Road or Racing Bike

Drop handlebars; skinny, high-pressure tires; narrow seat; 10 to 16 speeds. Fast but unstable ride. Low, stretched-out riding position for speed.

Touring and Sport Touring Bike

Similar to racing bikes, but designed for comfortable on-road use, bike tours, long distances, carrying gear. Slightly wider tire than a racing bike. Wide selection of gears, similar to a mountain bike. More relaxed frame geometry than a racing bike.

Track Bike

Similar to racing bikes, but designed only for track or velodrome use. Aerodynamic body position. One gear. No brakes.

David Epperson

City or Hybrid Bike

Looks like a mountain bike. First apparent difference is the narrower tire. Also known as cross bike, cross-terrain bike, cross-fitness bike. Combines features of road and mountain bikes. Suited for on-road use and limited off-road use. May be a good, inexpensive choice for recreational riders who will stay on pavement or very well-maintained dirt roads or paths.

Tandem Bike

Made as road or mountain bikes for two riders. A novelty. Consider price, safety, and bike transportation before purchase.

David Epperson

In a mountain bike, look for a relaxed geometric design that gives comfort and stability of ride, 1-3/4-inch to 2-1/2-inch wide tires that will give good traction and shock absorption, a wide gear selection for use in a variety of terrain, and cantilever brakes.

There are excellent, good, and not-so-good mountain bikes on the market. Consider frame materials, components, durability, weight, and serviceability when purchasing a mountain bike.

Remember the differences between mountain bikes and city or hybrid bikes. City bikes resemble mountain bikes in appearance but are not as strong and usually have narrower, less knobby tires and fewer gears. City and hybrid bikes begin at a lower price than do mountain bikes. If all of your riding will be on relatively flat pavement, and budget is a primary concern, a hybrid or city bike may be your best choice. If you plan to ride a variety of terrain, spend more for a mountain bike. You won't regret it.

As one of the world's fastest-growing sports and fitness activities, mountain biking is changing rapidly. There is much innovation. We've already seen the introduction (but not refinement) of the all-wheel-drive mountain bike. Other designers are working on collapsible mountain bikes that can be packed in a suitcase. New technology is making today's midpriced mountain bikes far superior to the top-of-the-line models of just a few years ago. Although today's mountain bike has opened a whole new world of adventure, there is no doubt we are still in the sport's infancy.

Take a Ride!

With the newfound freedom of this sturdy piece of equipment, you'll be able to escape the hurried rush of motor vehicles on the pavement of your community. You will become an authority on what lies at the end of each dirt road in the area. (One reminder: Good mountain bikers never trespass on private property.) You will reach new heights of mental and physical well-being, and you will experience fun and adventure as never before.

Is this your idea of outdoor enjoyment? Stop in at your local bicycle shop. Take a test ride. This is where the adventure begins.

David Epperson

Exploring off-road at Lake Catamount, Colorado.

The bicycle dates to the late 1700s and has clearly come a long way in its 200-year history. The mountain bike has been around only since the late 1970s and early 1980s. In its own way, it has come just as far.

Tom Ritchey, Gary Fisher, Charles Kelly, and others in Marin County, California, are generally credited with developing the mountain bike, starting out by gathering old bikes and using the parts to fashion a basic five-speed clunker.

Until this time, cycling's focus had been on youth bikes and the 10-speed, or road bike. But in the early 1980s, the mountain bike began to make rapid inroads into bicycle sales.

The wave of mountain biking spread from initial hotbeds in northern California and Colorado across the United States to Canada, Europe, Australia, New Zealand, and the Far East.

Within one short decade, the mountain bike became firmly established as the basic bicycle of adult Americans and accounted for a majority of the 11.6 million bicycles sold in the country. That's quite a jump from the total 1 million bicycles made in the United States during the so-called Bicycle Age year of 1899! This is indeed the Age of the Mountain Bike.

Mountain Bike Growth

According to the Bicycle Institute of America, more than 20 million Americans ride mountain bikes today, up from just 200,000 in 1983 and 2.6 million in 1986.

Just how much of the bicycle market the mountain bike will eventually capture is anybody's guess. In many small mountain towns and resort areas, mountain bikes already account for 90 percent or more of all full-size bicycle sales. Industry experts estimate that mountain bikes presently account for about two thirds of all full-size bicycle sales.

All the major bicycle manufacturers that have made road bikes, plus many others, are now making mountain bikes. There are about 20 major mountain bike manufacturers and literally hundreds of ''garage companies'' making custom, hand-built frames.

Membership in the National Off-Road Bicycle Association (NORBA), the U.S. mountain bike race sanctioning organization founded in 1983, demonstrates the sport's increasing popularity. In 1992, the group neared the 20,000 mark in membership and was asked to sanction about 500 races, up from 100 in just three years.

While most mountain bike competitors are 17 to 26 years old, NORBA officials point out that there are so many different kinds of people riding mountain bikes today it would be impossible to develop a profile of a typical mountain bike rider.

There's no one typical profile of a mountain biker.

The International Mountain Biking Association (IMBA) is perhaps the most representative group for mountain biking on an international level. It is dedicated to educating people on mountain biking as an environmentally sound and sustainable activity.

Based in Los Angeles, IMBA is affiliated with clubs across the United States, Canada, Italy, Finland, Spain, and Puerto Rico. IMBA receives industry support in North America, Europe, and Japan.

RIDING THE RUBICON TRAIL

This high country adventure had been in the back of my mind for years. A new invention called the mountain bike finally made it possible. On an August day in 1980, I rode a mountain bike across California's Sierra Nevada mountains, on the famed Rubicon Trail near Lake Tahoe.

Conditions were ideal. The pine-scented air, crystal-clear blue sky, and towering mountain peaks filled me with anticipation and a profound appreciation for the great outdoors. Early morning temperatures were mild, but would be warm before long.

A friend had driven me from my South Lake Tahoe home into the mountains, across Echo Summit, to my predetermined starting point, the tiny community of Riverton on Highway 50. We reviewed my route and the approximate time I hoped to return.

Saying good-bye, I gave my bike a final safety check and took a quick inventory of my essentials for the day. Everything seemed to be in order—helmet, spare tube, patch kit, tools, first-aid kit, sunscreen, and, of course, a topographic map with my route highlighted.

I was ready to ride, to begin the 60-mile (97-km) 1-day journey that is perhaps the most memorable ride I have taken in 30 years of bicycling.

The inspiration for this ride began abstractly about 10 years earlier. I was working at a lodge at Lake Tahoe and met a family who had just finished a 2-day jeep ride on what they described as the most beautiful four-wheel-drive road in the Sierra Nevada.

They had crossed the Rubicon Trail, a rugged and historic mountain crossing that over the years has become known for its annual jeep trek and as the ultimate proving ground for off-road vehicles.

At the time, I was a competitive cyclist, very much into training 60 to 120 miles (97 to 194 km) each day on my sleek road bike. Although the idea of the mountain bike never occurred to me, I remember being fascinated by the idea of cycling on rough mountain roads.

Donner Pass

Donner Lake

Truckee River

American River

Squaw Valley

French Meadow

Rubicon River

Hell Hole Res.

Loon Lake

Lake Tahoe

Buck Island Lake

Wentworth Springs

Cascade Lake

Union Valley Res.

RUBICON TRAIL

Desolation Valley

Crystal Basin

Wrights Lake

Fallen Leaf Lake

Ice House Lake

Riverton

Red Lake

Carson Pass

Silver Lake

Blue Lakes

Bear River Dam

So there I was 10 years later, ready to pedal off into a long-fantasized journey. With me was my first mountain bike, one of the first in the region, and I knew I had found the perfect place to try it out. As I climbed onto the saddle, I thought about the potential of this brand-new form of bicycling—the freedom, the outdoors, the excitement. To me, there was no doubt that this was bicycling's future.

I pedaled slowly as I warmed up along a deserted 20-mile (32-km) stretch of pavement that swept gently toward the towering Sierra crest. The warm sun and gorgeous terrain filled my senses. My first destination was Ice House Lake, the first of numerous lakes on my route.

Soon the shimmering waters of Ice House appeared as my first reward. I rode onward to Wentworth Springs and Loon Lake. Here the pavement ended and the mountain bike challenge of the Rubicon Trail began.

By about 11 a.m. I had pedaled 25 miles (40 km) along a beautiful country road. My first challenge was to locate the Rubicon trailhead. The map showed where the route began but the trail was not readily apparent. After carefully scanning the area, I decided this ride might be tougher than I had imagined.

I pushed and carried my bike up a steep ravine, which appeared to be the only probable route. Traces of black tire tracks and tiny oil stains on a few rocks were my only clues that vehicles had traveled this rugged path. When I finally emerged onto the ridge, I saw more of what appeared to be a trail. The area was very rough and during the first few miles, only chipped rock and tire traces on the granite slabs kept me on track.

As I reveled in this top-of-the-world wilderness, I still wasn't sure I was, in fact, on the Rubicon Trail. I hadn't seen a soul. I studied my map and rode on. I came upon small lakes that seemed to confirm I was on course. As I traveled on, the day warmed. I took breaks and swam in clear alpine lakes, enjoying their freshness and the solitude of high mountain meadows.

Finally, I saw a vehicle slowly moving toward me. I wondered how anyone could negotiate a vehicle across this steep route. The people in the vehicle were perhaps more amazed at how a bicycle could cross such terrain. At this time, most people had yet to see a mountain bike.

The jeepsters confirmed we were on the Rubicon Trail but suggested it would take me hours to ride the remaining 10 miles (16 km) to the shores of Lake Tahoe. It was 1 p.m. and I figured I could cover 10 miles by dark, even if I had to walk all the way. Even so, I curtailed the leisurely stops for swims and relaxation.

I pedaled with a renewed confidence. I actually caught and passed a few vehicles picking their way over the bumpy trail. I realized a bicycle could cover this terrain more gracefully than a motorized vehicle.

I rode harder, became more determined in my pace, and focused on the terrain with renewed intensity. The Rubicon was an ideal testing ground for a mountain bike; it tested all of my riding skills. Giant slabs of granite made some sections simple and fun. But then the trail would drop into ravines for true tests of riding ability.

Rocks of every shape and size cover the trail. Picking the right line and pedaling smoothly over obstacles is mountain biking at its best. Stream crossings abound as the Rubicon weaves its way over the mountains, and over every rise the view is spectacular. These are the reasons I have returned to this trail several times, bringing friends to share an unmatched experience.

After 16 miles (26 km) along the heart of the Rubicon, I crested the final ridge and could see the blue expanse of Lake Tahoe below me. I paused and felt satisfaction in my experiences of the day. Again I realized the magic in mountain biking.

By 6 p.m. I had not only descended to civilization along Lake Tahoe's shore, but also pedaled home to South Lake Tahoe, 20 paved miles (32 km) beyond the trailhead. I checked in with my friend, and as we talked about the ride, I began to realize this was only the beginning of my mountain bike discovery.

I thought about exploring endless trails, how mountain biking can open new opportunities for hikers and other outdoor enthusiasts, how it can bring year-round enjoyment and training to winter sports enthusiasts, how people of all ages would someday discover the mountain bike.

—Don Davis

2

MOUNTAIN BIKING EQUIPMENT

You will get more enjoyment from your mountain biking if you are equipped with the right gear. At the very least, you'll need a properly sized, well-maintained bike and a helmet. The helmet is an absolutely necessary piece of safety equipment.

Other frequently used items include sunglasses (for eye protection), cycling gloves (for padded grip and safety), a pair of padded bike shorts, and a water bottle. Accessories such as cycle computers are very popular. Additionally, you will probably need a vehicle rack to transport your bike to your riding destinations.

Beyond these basic items you will find wide ranges of mountain bike equipment and accessories that fill bike shops and mail-order catalogs around the world.

Where to Find the Right Bike

A comfortable bike of the correct size should be the first concern for the potential mountain biker. As with any other major purchase of specialized equipment, it pays to study up and shop around. Ask for recommendations from cycling friends and acquaintances, check out the cycling magazines, and watch for ads in your local newspapers.

Shopping for a Bike Shop

Where you buy your mountain bike is just as important as what kind of bike you buy, maybe even more so. When you begin to look for a mountain bike, you should first choose a bike shop, and consider several aspects.

In riding a bicycle, as in driving a car, you need access to professional advice, a good supply of parts, and a top-flight mechanic. This means the shop where you purchase your bike—and the shop where you will probably have it serviced—should be as close as possible to where you live or work. If you travel long distances to save a few dollars on a bicycle, will you be willing to travel again for parts, minor tune-ups, or adjustments?

Shop mechanics often hesitate to work on bikes bought elsewhere; they will advise you to visit the shop where you bought your bicycle. Of course, most mechanics are understandably reluctant to work on brands they are not familiar with.

As a consumer, you should feel confident your bike shop has knowledge-able sales and service personnel. Is it a full-service shop? Can it handle all your service needs, from fitting you properly at the original sale to possibly building a new wheel or aligning a damaged frame? Does the shop handle a wide range of bikes so you and your family can be satisfied now and in the future if you choose to upgrade?

Your shop should be able to satisfy all your equipment needs including good and timely service and parts ordering. If a part is not in stock, the shop should gladly special order it for you.

Buying at a nearby shop will make it easier for you to get your bike's 30-day after-purchase service as well as any subsequent tune-ups. The postpurchase service is provided free by reputable bike shops for nearly all major brands of bicycles and is perhaps the most important visit you will make to your bike shop after the original purchase.

A good shop's salespeople will listen to your needs and make appro-priate recommendations. If the salesperson isn't interested in listening

It's a good idea to buy your mountain bike from the shop where you expect to have it serviced.

and insists on telling you what to buy, consider it a warning to visit another bike shop. Sure, it's wise to take advantage of the salesperson's experience, but it should be on your terms.

CONSUMER TIP

Some shops may offer a 1-year or lifetime warranty on new mountain bikes. These are offered either as part of the purchase or as an extra-cost extended service contract. While good shops will back up this promise, others may use it only to attract your initial investment.

Long warranties have been used as a sales gimmick, causing the consumer to pay too much for the bike. The shop may be betting the buyer will forget or otherwise pass up the opportunity for extended service.

In any case, read the fine print on any shop warranties. Does the warranty cover wear and tear caused by regular use? Does it cover labor and parts? Find out what exactly it provides.

Test Rides and Rentals

There is no better way to select a bicycle than by taking a test ride. It's no different from selecting a new vehicle. Most bike shops will be happy to let you take a spin around the neighborhood, but be aware that in most cases you won't be able to take off-road test rides.

Many shops have demo models that you can rent and test off-road. And many of these shops will apply the rental charge to your eventual purchase price.

Mountain bike magazines (see appendix) feature regular reviews of various models of bikes. These provide lots of good information, but don't put all your faith in the reviews. Bike riders, like movie critics, have different preferences, and many of the reviews are geared to the more advanced rider.

One of the best ways to get a feel for differences in the many mountain bike models is to ride at one of the many ski resorts that have summertime mountain bike programs. They have good quality rental and demo bikes, usually in varying brands, models, and sizes. You may be able to attend

You can test-ride various mountain bikes on off-road conditions at a rental facility like this one.

a demo day where numerous brands and models will be available for test riding. Obviously, being able to compare different bikes on the same day in identical riding conditions can be of great help.

How to Choose a Mountain Bike

Before you go bike shopping, carefully consider your needs. Believe it or not, you can spend several thousand dollars for a fully equipped, top-of-the-line competition bike. Few of us need or can afford this kind of equipment. You should decide on a price range based on how often and where you plan to ride. This is important information. Your bike sales-person will ask these questions and then suggest options based on your plans and budget.

As in buying most specialized equipment, personal preference plays a major role in bicycle selection. Test-ride everything you can. Look for durability, light weight, index shifting, powerful brakes, and good ground clearance.

Underbuying is one of the most common mistakes made by the first-time bike buyer. You'll see an advertised special and buy the bike, perhaps from a large discount chain outlet, only to discover later that you need more than this heavy, entry-level clunker offers. Don't cut yourself short.

Price Ranges

How much should you pay for a mountain bike? If you try buying a cheap bike, you risk reduced satisfaction and increased chance of breakdown.

If you plan to stay on the pavement, you should be able to find a suitable hybrid or city bike for less than $300. Remember, the less-beefy city bikes won't handle tough off-road terrain.

If you plan some serious off-road riding, you should consider the $350 to $450 price range. This will buy a bike with a sturdy chro-moly steel frame and components that will stand up to most of the rigors of off-road riding.

In the $450 to $550 price range, you will step up to a more advanced frame geometry, perhaps other frame materials, and better components. You'll have a bike that shifts easier, brakes better, and perhaps has shock absorption. Your off-road experience will be more comfortable.

Moving into the advanced lines, from about $750 into the thousands of dollars, you will reach peak levels in high-tech function and durability. You will enjoy the exotic lightweight materials and top-of-the-line compo-nents used by the sport's top competitors.

■ FIND YOUR PRICE RANGE

Write next to each number below the letter that corresponds to how you'd most likely answer each of the following questions. When you're finished, score 1 point for every *a* answer, 2 for every *b*, and 3 for every *c*. Check the scoring key at the end of the questionnaire to find out the price range you should start looking in to find the kind of bike that will best fit your riding needs. Price ranges are in U.S. dollars.

1. How sure are you that mountain biking will become a regular part of your activity schedule?

   a. Not very. I just want to try the activity.
   b. Pretty sure.
   c. Very sure.

2. Where do you intend to ride?

   a. Mostly on-road.
   b. About the same on-road and off-road.
   c. Mostly off-road.

3. How many miles (kilometers) off-road do you think you'll ride each week?

   a. Under 15 miles (25 km).
   b. Fifteen to 30 miles (25-50 km).
   c. Over 30 miles (50 km).

Key

0-3 points, start looking in the $200 to $400 range
4-6 points, start looking in the $400 to $800 range
7-9 points, start looking in the $800 and up range

Bike Size and Reach

Buying the right size bike is the foremost consideration. Frame sizes start at about 16 inches (40.6 cm) for youths and range upward to about 23 inches (58.4 cm). Most adults use 20- or 21-inch (50.8- or 53.3-cm) mountain bikes with 26-inch wheels. Kid's sizes range from 16-inch (40.6-cm) frames with 20-inch wheels to 18-inch (45.7-cm) or so frames with 24-inch wheels.

Frame size is traditionally measured from the top of the seat tube to the center of the bottom bracket spindle.

A mountain bike is fitted to the rider in much the same way any other bike is fitted. But because you will be riding on bumpy, uneven terrain, you should have more clearance at the top tube. For mountain bikes, when you stand and straddle the top tube, you should have 2 to 4 inches (5 to 10 cm) of clearance between your crotch and the frame. If you plan to ride in very rough terrain, you may want added clearance for safety reasons.

Reach from seat to handlebar is a key factor in sizing and an important consideration for your riding comfort, as well as your ability to pedal with power. Generally your seat should be positioned about 2 inches (5 cm) higher than your handlebar. This allows for a dynamic body position with more power, better weight distribution, and proper leverage when climbing.

A bike that is too big can take you for a ride—it can be dangerous and difficult to handle and could possibly lead to a serious accident. Conversely, a bike that is too small will give you a cramped feeling, and you won't be comfortable or efficient in your riding.

If you are uncertain in your knowledge of bike size, frame material, the bike's working condition, or price, shop with someone who is more familiar with mountain biking. They can help you determine value and give you a better chance of scoring a great deal.

Opportunities for finding good, previously owned mountain bikes are getting better all the time. Riders are moving up to higher quality models and young people are moving up to larger frames, creating a pool of used mountain bikes for people of all ages.

Used mountain bikes are found in bicycle shops, through ads on bike shop or school or college bulletin boards, and through local classified ads. Some of the more populated regions have shops or publications specializing in used cycles and cycling and sports equipment.

There are great buys to be found if you know what you are looking for. Compare prices and features with new models on the market. You can expect a good mountain bike to depreciate in value by 10 percent to 20 percent per year and then level out in the $200 to $400 range.

You should have 2 to 4 inches (5 to 10 cm) of clearance between crotch and frame.

Frames

Today's mountain bike frames are made of many different materials, some very sophisticated and each with its own advantages. Steel remains the industry standard frame material.

High-tensile or high-carbon steels are generally heavier and not as strong as chrome-molybdenum (chro-moly). These types of steel are usually found in the most inexpensive mountain bikes and should be avoided if you plan to leave the pavement.

Most steel-frame mountain bikes are TIG (tungsten inert gas) welded. This type of welding can be recognized by the rough appearance of the weld at a joint. The other way of joining tubes or adding fittings is brazing. This is usually done with silver or brass. A lug is usually used to attach tubes with the brazing process.

Steel-frame bikes are the most popular because of their cost, durability, comfort, and service life.

You will find other materials in mountain bike frames including aluminum, carbon fiber, and titanium.

But, the first-time buyer will probably be happiest with a double-butted chro-moly frame. Always keep in mind that proper design, fit, assembly, and adjustment are much more important than frame materials in the bike's overall feel and performance.

AT A GLANCE: FRAME MATERIALS

	Advantages	*Disadvantages*	*Dollar range*
Chro-moly steel	Strength and stiffness Ease of repair Low price	Weight Rougher ride	$200-$1,500
Aluminum	Light weight Smooth ride Responsiveness	Greater variation in ride qualities Difficulty of repair	$600-$3,000
Carbon fiber	Light weight Smooth ride Responsiveness	Fragility to certain impacts Cost of repair	$800-$3,000
Titanium	Strength Responsiveness Durability	High cost	$2,000 and up

Component Choices

Bicycle components, primarily shifters and derailleurs and brake levers and brakes, are a chief factor in bicycle pricing. Ask your bike shop about the differences in components from various manufacturers. A select few large component makers dominate the field internationally. Each makes several lines or groups of components.

Gears and Brakes

Check the feel of various shifters and brake levers, which vary in size, shape, and speed of function. Do you prefer the motorcycle feel of a grip shifter to the standard thumb shifter? Ask about features such as Shimano's

Frame Materials

Chro-moly Steel

If you plan to ride off-road, your steel frame should be chro-moly (cr-mo) steel throughout, including frame and forks and it should be double-butted. If you hear the terms triple-butted or quad-butted, these are even stronger. Butting is the process that makes the tube walls thicker at the ends than in the middle, giving the greatest strength at the joints. The tubes taper off to a thinner wall in the middle, saving weight. Triple- or quad-butted frames have three or four different thicknesses within the tube, rather than just two.

David Epperson

Aluminum Tubing

David Epperson

Weight is the greatest advantage of aluminum; it is three times lighter than steel. It is weaker and more flexible, depending on diameter and tube wall thickness. Thus, when you look at aluminum bikes you will often see over-sized tubing for greater strength. After matching the strength of steel in an aluminum bike you will usually wind up with a frame weight savings of 10 percent to 20 percent. The aluminum frame will save weight, and it can provide a stiffer or softer ride, depending on tubing size and design goals of the manufacturer.

David Epperson

Carbon Fiber

These are composite man-made materials of glass carbon, polyester, or carbon. The fibers are glued, usually with epoxy, and layered for strength. Carbon fiber frames are molded to achieve proper strength and ridability. This material holds great promise but is expensive. Carbon fiber does save some weight but has yet to prove durable enough for rugged mountain bike use.

David Epperson

Titanium Tubing

Glamorous and expensive, it doesn't rust and doesn't need paint. Used in satellites and aircraft, titanium is the most exotic material used in mountain bike construction. It weighs 40 percent less than steel and is reported to be as strong as any chro-moly. Titanium comes closest to matching steel in all respects and is better in durability and service life. However, titanium is very expensive and will probably stay that way in the near future.

Hyperglide which smooths your shifting. Remember that there is a huge aftermarket and these and other components can be changed later if you like.

Suspension

The mountain bike rage of the '90s has been suspension, a feature now offered by nearly every mountain bike manufacturer. Most companies use shock absorbing suspension forks in the front, some offer rear suspension, and others have come up with various futuristic designs. Initial concerns about increased weight versus performance have been alleviated by the introduction of new front shocks that add very little to total bike weight.

Shock absorbers need to react at high and low speeds; therefore, adjustable models may be better. Look for shocks with easy access for on-the-trail adjustment. Suspension is most cost-effective when purchased on a new bike; retrofitting remains expensive, although costs are coming down.

Nearly every mountain bike racer is now using suspension but not all riders agree it is necessary. Test-ride a suspension-equipped bike and decide for yourself.

Front shocks.

Handlebars

Width is a consideration. You want your hands to be spread comfortably. Bar ends can be attached to the handlebars to create an alternative hand position.

DO YOU NEED SHOCK ABSORBERS?

I ride an Allsop bike, which has been one of the more unusual looking bikes on the market in recent years. The Allsop Softride Suspension System is different from most suspension systems. It suspends the rider rather than the bike.

Other systems use shock absorbers on the front forks and maybe in the stem and rear, but the Allsop system places the saddle on a resin-molded carbon fiber suspension beam that is attached in front to the frame. It also features a shock-absorbing stem. It's unique and may look odd, but I find that it provides high levels of comfort and performance.

Suspension in mountain bikes is at the stage of innovation and debate. Manufacturers have been taking cues from the motorcycle industry in developing their suspension technologies.

Although many bikes come stock with suspension, the concept still has a long way to go. The first-time buyer should consider components and frame first and not place too much emphasis on suspension.

—Don Davis

Stem

This part attaches your handlebar to the headset. Look for a lightweight stem with a shape that gives you a comfortable position and reach from seat to handlebar. Shock absorbing stems are also available.

Crankset

Your cranks attach your pedals to the crankset. Large, round chainrings provide smooth spinning. Many bikes are equipped with out-of-round inner rings for power pedaling.

Pedals

New riders may stick with the standard bicycle pedal, but in rough terrain a standard pedal may allow the foot to slip, causing a lower body collision with the top tube. You may want to add toe clips. Once you get the hang of flipping into your clips, you'll wonder how you rode without them. Many advanced riders use clipless pedals that, when used with compatible cycling shoes, offer precise control through step-in entry and quick release, like a ski binding.

Wheels, Spokes

Mountain bike wheels and spokes are designed for heavy-duty use. You shouldn't have to worry about wobbly or dinged wheels.

Tires

Bicycle tires have different tread designs with the knobby, high-traction mountain bike tire at one end of spectrum and the skinny, high-speed road tire at the other. Look for wide lugs on the side of the tread to help in cornering at speed and for mud release. Most riders use identical front and rear tires but some will use a front tire designed for more steering control. Some tire makers offer specially designed front and rear tires. There are cross tires designed for both road and off-road riding.

Saddle

Your mount won't give you a lot of pleasure if it isn't saddled with a comfortable seat. Look first at the saddle size, shape, and width. Compare it to your size, shape, and width. Anatomy comes first. If standard padding doesn't cut it, there are several fine, self-molding saddles on the market. Gel-like substances, flow liquids, and fluids are designed into saddles. The idea is to equalize pressure, reduce pressure points, and provide a softer cushion.

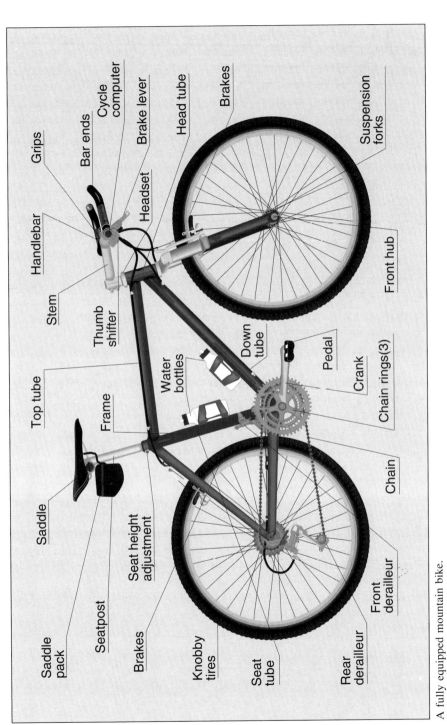

A fully equipped mountain bike.

Getting the Right Safety Gear, Apparel, and Accessories

To ride comfortably and successfully, a mountain biker needs more than just a well-equipped bike. Safety gear is essential, and the right clothing and accessories make riding more enjoyable.

Suiting Up for Safety

You need to make sure you have the necessary gear to ride safely. Protecting yourself from injuries as a result of spills or from the effects of the sun will allow you to concentrate on enjoying your ride.

Helmets

The helmet is unquestionably the mountain biker's most important piece of safety gear. To emphasize the importance of head protection, many bike shops are including helmets, helmet discounts, or other incentives with the purchase of a mountain bike. In any case, you should make sure a helmet is part of your overall bicycle budget. A "brain bucket" could save your life and should be considered a mandatory piece of equipment. It is among the best investments you can make to ensure a long and healthy life of mountain biking.

A helmet's main purpose is to reduce harmful effects of a blow to the head. Today's helmets are safe, sturdy, and lightweight, with most models weighing just 8 or 9 ounces (227 or 255 g). Expanded polystyrene (EPS) is the energy-absorbing material of which most helmets are made. A smaller number of helmets are made from expanded polypropylene. Helmets are covered with a thin plastic shell, hard plastic shell, or Lycra. Generally, the hard-shell models have been considered tougher and the foam models lighter. All good helmets will meet ANSI and SNELL safety standards. Modern helmets are often computer-designed to provide better fit and ventilation and reduced wind resistance.

Look for comfort, fit, light weight, ventilation, durability, and removable, adjustable padding. Quick release buckles are standard. Bright coloring will make you more visible to motorists (you can also pick up brightly colored and inexpensive helmet covers).

Helmet prices range from about $40 to $150, less for youngsters and more for top-rated competition models with features such as pump airflow fitting.

AT A GLANCE: HELMET SURFACES

	Advantages	Disadvantages	Dollar range
Hard plastic	Very durable. Prevents penetration of sharp objects	Slightly heavier	$30-$60
Thin plastic	Attractive, durable, light, easy to clean	None	$40-$150
Lycra	Less expensive, can change cover	Harder to keep clean, can snag on limbs and branches	$30-$60

Helmets are available to fit every rider.

Wear your helmet and show your children, by example, the importance of head protection. Cyclists suffer far too many head injuries, and of those injuries 75 percent are in children younger than 15.

Even in this enlightened age, you may hear some cyclists suggest that helmets are hot, uncomfortable, and unnecessary. Don't believe it. You'll get used to your helmet quickly and it will be part of your everyday ride.

■ FIT YOUR HELMET PROPERLY

For proper safety, it is imperative that your helmet fit snugly. Follow these steps to make sure the fit of your helmet is correct.

1. Place the helmet on your head so that it rests low on the brow to protect your forehead.
2. Adjust the straps so they form a *Y* in front of and below the ear. The chin strap should fit well under the chin and against the neck to be as snug as possible. This will ensure that your helmet stays in place when you need it most.

3. With the helmet fastened, push the helmet backward and forward, side to side. If the skin on your brow moves with the helmet and if the helmet moves only slightly, the fit is good.

Eye Protection

Eye protection is often underrated in terms of safety. Serious eye injuries can occur to cyclists who do not use eye protection. One of the most serious is damage from the sun's ultraviolet rays. Most of today's modern cycling and skiing glasses offer 100 percent UV protection.

Another reason for wearing glasses is to protect your eyes from foreign objects such as rocks coming off your tires, insects, and branches of trees or bushes.

The best sunglasses are optically true. They should also be made of an unbreakable and scratch-resistant material. Glasses that resemble goggles afford the most wind and weather protection. These glasses help protect the eye from flying objects, no matter what the angle.

Skin Protection

Cyclists should be concerned about skin protection. A good sunblock with a sun protection factor (SPF) of 15 is advisable. The best sunblocks are water resistant. Put the sunblock on 15 to 20 minutes before going into the sun. If necessary, plan on more than one application if you will be out for more than an hour in sunny weather.

Also keep in mind that a good moisturizer for the skin is important both before and after rides. The sun and wind can have a definite aging effect which moisturizers can help alleviate.

Gloves

Cycling gloves are used for safety and comfort. A good cycling glove can help protect your hands from abrasions if you fall, and padded gloves will help absorb road shock. If your hands have a tendency to numb while riding (a common occurrence), you may want to look into gloves with a petroleum based, gel-like material to better absorb shock. Gloves will also help protect against blisters and calluses. Use fingerless models for most riding and full-finger gloves in cold weather.

Look for durable, machine-washable gloves with heavy-duty palms and reinforced thumb pads, in either leather or synthetics, with Velcro closures. Some gloves have a sewn-in terry cloth brow wipe, which is a very handy feature.

Apparel

Fashion is in, of course, and cycling clothing offers plenty of style. But while shopping, remember that cycle apparel is designed primarily for function. It pads you, protects you, and keeps you cool or warm, dry and comfortable, in sweltering or subfreezing conditions.

In cycling, the effects of changing temperatures can be dramatic. You may overheat on a long climb only to chill on a long, shaded descent. Sweat can turn to dampness, chill, and even hypothermia (a lowering of the body temperature). Rain and cold weather can put a damper on your riding if you're not properly attired. In winter, frostbite can affect the extremities. If you ride year-round, proper cycling apparel becomes a necessity.

As in other active outdoor endeavors, layering is the key to good cycling dress. A single summer layer is replaced by perhaps two layers during the changing seasons and three during the cold winter months.

DRESSING FOR SUCCESS

Bike Shorts and Tights

Bike shorts will probably become your first item of cycling apparel after a few hard days in the saddle. Tights serve the same purpose, but are used in colder temperatures to cover the entire leg. Both are usually made to fit the bent-leg cycling position. Look for comfort, durability, multipanel design, ample padding around the crotch, and heavy-duty stitching on either stretch Lycra (with leg gripper material to keep the short from riding up) or the baggy, mountain-bike-style short. Cycling shorts and tights have a longer rise than exercise garments for comfort and coverage in the cycling position. As an alternative, try padded cycling briefs (for men and women); then you can wear any shorts or pants and still enjoy a padded ride.

Shoes

Cycling shoes have a stiffer sole to put more power into your pedaling. Mountain bike shoes have a hiking-boot-style tread pattern for those times you must push or carry your bike. Many of the new cycling shoes for mountain biking and road biking are designed for use with either toe clip or step-in (clipless) pedals.

Jerseys and Jackets

Look for a garment that wicks moisture away from the skin (such as polypropylene, CoolMax, etc.). Modern materials allow cooling in hot weather yet preserve body heat in colder temperatures. Outside, you'll want rain and wind protection (Gore-Tex, Supplex, etc.). A long tail cut in back and longer sleeves provide body coverage in the bent-over riding position. Velcro closures, easy-to-reach pockets, venting, and bright colors are added features. Many cycling garments have sewn-in reflective materials to increase visibility.

All-Weather Suits

Look for Gore-Tex or a similar proven all-weather material. Multi-purpose suits should be fully ventilated with underarm zippers and back vents to control the amount of heat and vapor that will escape.

Look for long tails on the jacket, a high waist on the pants, leg zippers, and Velcro cuff closures.

A relatively mild day can bring a windchill factor of freezing if the wind is blowing briskly. Bundling up with heavy clothes is not the answer; your clothing can become wet or sweat-soaked. You can stay warm and dry by layering. It is important to have an undergarment that wicks moisture away from the skin. Your middle layer provides insulation, and your outer shell provides wind and rain protection. Materials such as Gore-Tex and Ultrex are breathable to wick away moisture yet provide excellent water repellency.

Remember, you can lose up to 40 percent of your body heat through your head. Headbands or ski hats can be worn under the helmet. A helmet cover can provide some protection. Use full-fingered, windproof, and waterproof cycling gloves. Too much glove padding (such as in ski gloves) can affect your ability to shift and brake. Use socks or neoprene covers (booties) over your cycling shoes. Stow away some polypropylene arm and leg warmers to pull on when the weather changes quickly.

Accessories

If your riding takes you more than walking distance from civilization, you should consider certain accessories for your mountain bike. In addition to basic items such as a water bottle, you may need a pump, patch kit, spare tire tube, and basic tools including Allen wrenches and a small crescent wrench. Remember, flat tires are by far the most common backcountry breakdown mountain bikers face.

Water Bottles

A water bottle is the most common mountain bike accessory. In fact, many bikes come equipped with a water bottle cage attached to the frame. Many riders carry two bottles. Cages are made of various materials and new configurations are being introduced. Oversized cages will hold larger, 1.5-liter bottles for thirsty riders or long trips. Some riders use specially made belts or backpacks with a water bottle pocket; some have straws so you can sip and still keep both hands on your bars. Insulated underseat packs are made to keep water bottles cold.

Pumps

Mountain bikers often prefer mini-pumps that can be attached to the down tube or top tube of the frame. One manufacturer has even designed a pump that is built into a sliding seat post. The larger, full-size pumps may pump more air per stroke but they are less handy. Hand-sized inflating devices that use replaceable CO_2 (carbon dioxide) cartridge refills can be used by the rider who wants to keep gear at a minimum. These can be carried in a pack or clipped to the frame. Good pumps are equipped for use with both Presta and Schrader valves. Look for durability, ease of use, and easy mounting.

Packs

Most popular is the seat pack which mounts under your saddle and is used for your tools, patch kit, and day-ride items. For the rider who wants to pack more or for the tourer, there are handlebar bags (some come with map mounts), panniers (paired for balanced load) for front and rear, and triangular frame bags that can carry small items and double as shoulder padding when you carry your bike. In all cycling packs, look for durable materials, balance, convenience, and easy access.

Luggage Racks

Without a rack, anything sizable is difficult to transport on a bicycle. It takes both hands and feet to ride safely. For trips to the post office or corner store, a rack is a nice addition. Look for strength, light weight, and the ability to carry a balanced load. Racks come in front and rear models. A rear rack should be used first; add a front rack for touring. Some newer racks come equipped with convenient built-in cargo straps, and some racks also offer mud protection.

Cycle Computers

Using a cycle computer adds a whole new dimension to your riding and training. You can time your rides and measure trip distance, total distance, current speed, and maximum speed. Better models also measure cadence and average speed (to let you know whether you're at your desired training level). Some also have altimeters that will show elevation changes on your ride. The latest, top-end models have built-in heart rate monitors.

Most models include clock, stopwatch, odometer, and speedometer (adjustable to miles or kilometers per hour) and automatic on/off. Cadence, altimeter, and heart rate functions are found in the pricier models.

Look for size of display, ease of use, watertightness, and light weight. Beware of wireless models; these may work well on road bikes but

Distribute your supplies evenly in panniers for comfortable touring.

sometimes don't stand up in rough off-road riding. In cycle computers, you can generally expect to get what you pay for. The expensive models work very well; the inexpensive models may be confusing to operate, inaccurate in measurement, and short-lived.

Mirrors

Safe riders are aware of their surroundings. Small mirrors that attach to the end of the handlebar and can be tucked away in tight riding conditions are among the best choices. Some riders prefer tiny models that attach to the helmet or eyeglasses.

Lights

With more night riding and mountain bike commuting, demand has increased for lights. Off-road lighting began with helmet lights similar to those used by coal miners, and they are still popular. Today's lighting choices are much wider and include battery-powered halogen headlamps and flashing or constant taillights. The lamps are clamped to the bike; the battery is either mounted to the frame or carried in a custom seat pack. Look for long-life rechargeability, weathertightness, and adjustability.

Mud Guards

If much of your riding is on muddy roads or trails, then, by all means, pick up some mud guards. They will prevent your legs, back, and usually your face from being splattered.

SAFETY TIP   If you plan to ride in remote areas, you should be prepared to deal with any emergencies that may occur.

Compact first-aid kits can be purchased at cycling, sporting goods, auto parts, or camping and outdoor stores. They include basic materials to treat minor cuts and bruises and insect bites. Small kits will fit in a bag under your saddle.

3

MOUNTAIN BIKING CORRECTLY

The rewards of mountain biking are measured in many ways. One of the most satisfying is in adapting your riding style to the challenges that nature presents to you—in using the terrain for a graceful, flowing ride, no matter what the obstacles. This gives a sense of accomplishment and a oneness with your surroundings. Like the skier or sailor, the mountain biker picks a line and blends his or her movement to the challenge at hand.

Mountain biking is easy to learn; with practice, its techniques become instinctive. If you have ridden a bicycle, skillful mountain biking is mainly a matter of learning shifting, braking, and weight distribution techniques and, of course, developing a sufficient fitness level.

Like the powder skiers who carve graceful arcs in fresh snow, experienced mountain bikers embody grace and elegance as they put their unique touches on the landscape.

IFA Bilderteam/Leo de Wys

Meeting the challenges of nature.

Mathis/Zefa/H. Armstrong Roberts

Covering the terrain in good form.

Basic Braking, Shifting, and Body Position

On your first mountain bike ride, you will begin—as a matter of necessity—to develop the basic skills of braking and shifting. It's not hard to squeeze your brake levers or click your shifters, but it takes time and practice to learn the secrets of stopping powerfully and in balance on varied terrain or shifting fluidly at just the right time to carry the proper speed through a change in the trail.

Braking

The power of standard mountain bike cantilever brakes is limited mainly by how much energy it takes to use the brake lever. The cycling industry is developing many innovations in brakes. Self-energizing, hydraulic, and cam brake systems are being improved and may become more widely used in coming years. Much attention is being paid to advances such as these because more efficient braking will make off-road biking even more safe and enjoyable than it is today.

In braking, the general rule is to use the rear brake first. Too much pressure on the front brake could toss you onward without your bike. Also be aware of which hand controls which brake. Standard bikes are set up so the right hand controls the rear brake and the left hand controls the front brake. This works because the natural tendency for a right-handed person is to squeeze the rear brake first. Be sure to check any used bikes because some riders, mostly left-handers, do change the pattern because of personal preference. For simplicity's sake, southpaws can and should quickly get used to the standard brake setup.

Of course, using front and rear brakes together gives you the best stopping power. It must be emphasized, however, that too much front brake use can pitch you forward, so it is good to practice a slight rearward shift of the body as you increase pressure on the front brake. The rear brake is especially valuable in controlling speed at slower speeds, but above about 15 mph (24 kph), the rear brake may not stop you quickly enough on its own.

Practice brake use on a safe, level area to find the combination of stopping power that feels best for you. Make sure you can comfortably reach both brake levers and squeeze them effectively. Brake levers can be adjusted for reach so a person with a small hand can get a good grip, even on a large lever.

Practice routine stops and then work up to quicker stops. Avoid skidding except for an occasional test of your rear brake adjustment; your lever should be adjusted so you can lock and skid the rear wheel without the brake lever touching the handlebar.

Most brakes have barrel adjustments near the lever that can be easily used to set proper tension. You should also check to make sure your brake pads, front and rear, are hitting evenly on the rim and not rubbing on the tire. This can cause unnecessary tire damage.

Practice braking in all terrain and conditions. Remember that wet rims will inhibit stopping power by 10 to 30 percent so use extra caution in damp conditions. The idea is to be prepared to slow down or stop quickly in all conditions and in any emergency.

■ PRACTICE SAFE BRAKING

1. Find a safe, level area for braking practice. Start by practicing routine stops, then work up to quicker stops.
2. When you decide to stop, gently squeeze the rear brake first with your right hand.
3. Within a split second, gently squeeze the front brake lever with your left hand while shifting your weight slightly to the rear of the bike.
4. Remember that too much front brake might pitch you forward but that the back brake alone at speeds over 15 mph (24 kph) won't stop you quickly enough.

EARTH WATCH   The most serious environmental scars mountain bikers leave on trail systems occur when the rider skids his or her rear wheel in braking. Trail damage is also caused by riding during or right after a rain.

Good mountain bikers avoid causing erosion and unnecessary roughness on the trail. This is a growing concern among organized mountain bike groups, other trail users, and environmentalists.

Learn to brake and stop at a point just short of skidding. This is the most efficient way to apply the brakes, and it is much easier on nature.

Shifting

Shifting gears takes more practice than braking. Most mountain bikes have 15, 18, 21, or 24 speeds, so you will have plenty of choices. Your legs and gears together are like your car's transmission; they turn smoothly, at different cadences, depending on speed and terrain. Always keep pedaling as you shift gears. Smooth pedaling leads to smooth shifting.

Mountain bike gear-shifters are located so you can shift safely and easily without lifting your hands from the handlebar. There are different styles of shifters—including thumb-shift levers, push-button or rapid-fire shifters, and grip shifters in which the hand grip turns (like on a motorcycle throttle)—but all accomplish the same basic function: moving the chain from one chainring to another.

If you have thumb levers, think of shifting as clockwise and counter-clockwise motions. To upshift you move your shifters clockwise, to down-shift you move them counterclockwise (more on changing gears in a few paragraphs). This goes for either hand; think of your handlebar as the face of a clock, or a steering wheel.

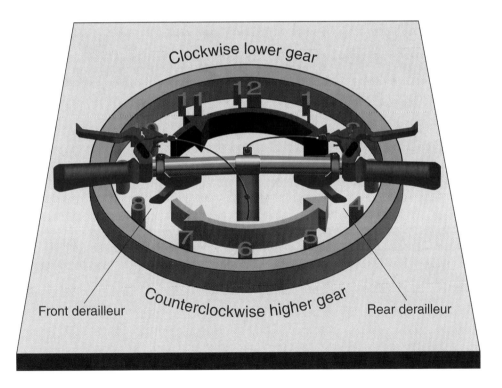

Thumb levers.

Push-button or rapid-fire shifters are featured on many of today's mountain bikes. Some of the most convenient models use a push-push system—one button for upshifting and the other for downshifting. One push, one gear. Others combine thumb buttons with trigger-style finger levers and a push-pull style. The one-gear-at-a-time movement of the button shifter can be viewed as an advantage or a disadvantage, depending on how you ride.

Grip shifters allow riders to change gears by turning the handlebar grip in a style popular for motorcycles. This is an increasingly popular feature on mountain bikes.

Whatever the style of your shifters, your left-hand shifter controls the derailleur on the large chainrings in the front. As you shift away from you (clockwise), you shift up through the gears, moving from smaller to larger chainrings. Your right-hand shifter controls your rear derailleur. As you click the shifter toward you (again clockwise), you shift from the larger to the smaller cogs for the higher gear.

It is easiest to pedal and climb when your chain is on the small chainring in front (left hand). The small chainring is used for steeps and slower speeds. The middle ring offers a midrange, and the large ring is for high speed (over 20 mph or 32 kph). In off-road use, many mountain bikers will not use the large chainring. The higher the gear, the harder it is to pedal.

Use your rear gears (right hand) in combination with your front chainrings to select ranges of gearing. You will quickly decide on a few combinations that feel most comfortable and productive for you.

Try to shift one gear at a time in most instances. Always try to shift front first, then rear as you seek a lower gear. To prepare for a sharp change in terrain, you may occasionally wish to shift two or three gears at a time. But avoid going from the largest gear to the smallest all at once. Shifting through too many gears at one time can cause too much chain tension or chain slap. At advanced levels of riding it may be necessary to shift front and rear simultaneously. Remember, though, the biggest mistake beginners make is bogging down by pedaling too slow in too high a gear.

Practice your shifting. At first, use an open, flat area; a parking lot is ideal. Become aware of the range of gears and learn to shift at the optimum time. Downshift as you approach a climb so you don't lose speed. Try downshifting while pedaling in the standing position. Work on timing; if you downshift too early you will lose momentum at the beginning of the climb. The reverse holds true as you crest a hill. Practice upshifting as the trail levels or drops downhill.

If you've been riding a 10-speed or other older bike and didn't like the inconvenient or confusing shifting, you'll love your mountain bike. The index shifting found on most mountain bikes gives you a clear gear change with every click of the shifter; you'll be able to shift while steering; and you'll always know what gear you're in.

Many of the mountain bike's multiple gears overlap. You probably won't use all the gears, but it's nice to know they are there when you need them.

For a typical climb, use your small chainring with the top three or four cogs in the rear. For mild, rolling rides, use your middle chainring with all the rear cogs. On a fast flat or downhill, you might use your large chainring with the smallest three or four cogs in the rear. As you consider what gear to use, think in terms of cadence, of keeping your pedals spinning at a consistent rate.

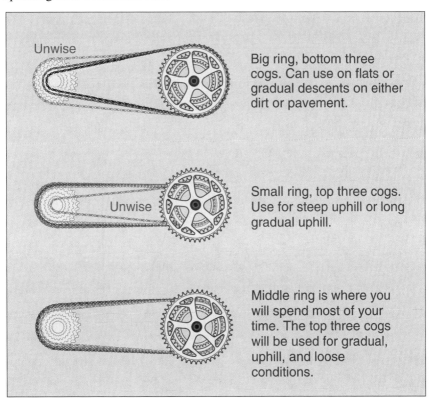

Unwise

Big ring, bottom three cogs. Can use on flats or gradual descents on either dirt or pavement.

Unwise

Small ring, top three cogs. Use for steep uphill or long gradual uphill.

Middle ring is where you will spend most of your time. The top three cogs will be used for gradual, uphill, and loose conditions.

Gears.

■ LEARN TO SHIFT EFFICIENTLY

With practice, you'll soon learn how to find the gear that works best for the terrain you're riding. While you're learning, remember these tips.

1. Shift one gear at a time, shifting the front first, then rear.
2. As you approach an ascent, you should move from the larger chainring to the smaller. Upshift as you approach a descent.
3. Maintain a consistent pedal cadence as you shift gears.

Body Position

Frame size, seat height, and reach each have an effect on basic body position and comfort on the mountain bike. Your bike should not be too big. Be sure you can straddle the bike's top tube with comfortable clearance; experts often will recommend 2 inches (5 cm) of clearance if you plan on-road riding and up to 4 inches (10 cm) for off-road riding. A more general rule of thumb is 2 inches (5 cm) of clearance for a recreational rider and 4 inches (10 cm) for a more aggressive or competitive rider.

■ ADJUST YOUR SADDLE HEIGHT

The optimal saddle height depends on whether you are pedaling normally or descending a steep hill. Some riders lower their seat a few inches on tough descents for safety and stability. Because most mountain bikes are equipped with quick-release seat posts, you can quickly slide your saddle up or down as the terrain dictates. To adjust your saddle height to the optimal position for pedaling normally, use this process:

1. Sit on the seat.
2. Loosen the seat post and slide it up until your leg is outstretched with your heel on the pedal.
3. Make sure that your leg is slightly bent when the ball of your foot is centered on the pedal.

Proper reach will put you in a comfortable, powerful position, neither too outstretched nor too upright, with arms slightly bent, not locked. In the riding position, your back should be at about a 45-degree angle. To accomplish this position, your handlebar will be slightly lower than your

The handlebars should be slightly lower than the seat; this should put your back at a 45-degree angle.

saddle. As you bend over into a more aggressive position, you have more leverage and balance. If you sit too straight, you may sacrifice power.

Depending on how aggressively you ride, you may want to experiment with the height and length of your handlebar stem. Raising the stem will put you in a more upright position, which is usually more comfortable but less powerful. Lowering the stem will lower your upper body and probably reduce your comfort but give you more leverage and power. Lower-priced bikes will usually have higher stems and more upright riding positions. More expensive bikes, especially competition models, will have lower stems to distribute the rider's weight forward for leverage, power, and control.

Riding Uphill

Uphill riding skills involve shifting, weight distribution, balance, and momentum. You must be able to judge degrees of steepness, surface conditions, and obstacle clearance.

■ HANDLE CLIMBS EFFECTIVELY

The first thing to remember as you approach a hill is to shift down into a smaller gear well ahead of time, before you roll to a stop. It's not necessary to shift all the way down, but knowing you can get down into the right gear is important. Plan ahead and you won't lose momentum when you really need it. Here's how to approach a hill with confidence:

1. When you're almost to the hill, first shift off of your big chainring in front to the middle chainring with your left hand.
2. Glance down between your feet to check which ring your chain is on, then quickly look back to the trail.
3. If things look steep, shift again, this time from the middle to the small chainring.
4. If pedal speed is dropping, shift your rear derailleur into one of the middle cogs with your right hand. Keep shifting down until you find the right gear for you.
5. Don't wait too long to change gears. Shifting becomes more difficult as pedal speed drops.
6. Keep your weight balanced by bending at the waist and elbows to shift some of your weight over the front wheel while you're seated.
7. Watch for rocks, ruts, or other obstacles so you can plan ahead for proper pedal clearance.

Your effort should be based on how long the hill appears to be. When climbing, it is wiser to choose too small a gear than too large. In a low gear, your feet will spin rapidly, but this uses less energy than pushing harder in a higher gear.

In the proper gear, you can prepare for the tough part of the climb. Concentration is important in two ways. You must believe you are going to stay on your bike to the top of the hill and, depending on the terrain, you must look ahead for the proper line. This simply means that if there are rocks, ruts, curbs, or a combination of these, you must choose the easiest and most ridable line. Concentrate on what is directly ahead of you, yet glance beyond as well. Plan ahead and you will avoid coming to a sudden stop.

Weight Distribution

When climbing a steep hill, you must balance your weight properly. Normally, you will be seated as you climb. This means your weight will

Bend your arms and press some weight forward to prevent tipping over backward when going uphill.

be over the rear wheel to maintain good traction. At the same time, you must keep the front of the bike weighted. This is done partly by flattening your back and bending your elbows to press weight forward. Being too far back could cause the front wheel to rise and even cause you to tip over backward.

If you find it necessary to stand up for more power as you climb a hill, you may have to shift your weight back some to maintain traction. By slightly shifting your weight up and back you will find the position that will allow you to stand and pedal without breaking traction.

It is always a challenge to see whether you can stay on the bike as you go up a very steep trail, but remember, those slow-motion falls can really hurt! If it looks too steep, plan ahead and get off and walk. Many riders have fallen hard because they were stubborn and waited too long to dismount.

The idea is to have fun and enjoy yourself, not to accidentally roll off a steep embankment. Keep this in mind and know your limitations.

Pedal Clearance

It's important to know your pedal clearance. When your pedal is down you have very limited ground clearance. If you are riding over a rock, rut, or other obstacle be careful not to bury your pedal. This can lead to another slow motion fall and damage to you, your bike, or both.

Some hills require a short burst of pedal speed so that you will be able to put your pedal in the proper horizontal position to make it over a tricky obstacle. Also, because most hills have one or several steep pitches, you may need to pedal quickly to negotiate the steep parts, then rest on the flatter sections.

Thoughts on Climbing

Make sure you are completely in gear before you put maximum load on the pedals. Try to remain seated when climbing steep, loose sections. Standing up in loose areas is a sure way to lose traction and come to an unnecessary stop.

Keep in mind that wet tires, rocks, and wood are very slippery. Having a little less air pressure in your tires will give better traction. Keeping your toe clip straps a little loose or the tension light on clipless pedals when climbing hills will help you dismount quickly and smoothly.

It helps to take a hill little by little. That is, don't come to the base of a climb and look way up to the top and say, "I know I can't make this hill." Surprise yourself by taking it one short section at a time. Before you know it, you'll be at the top. But always remember, hills will get your heart pumping in a hurry. Pay attention to your body. If your heart is pounding in your ears, it's probably time to get off and walk or rest.

The main points to remember in climbing: Shift early so you will be in a low gear as you ride to the first steep pitch; keep your weight evenly distributed and stay seated on the really steep sections for better traction; slide back in the saddle for better leverage and traction; pick the proper line; watch your pedal clearance; anticipate when it is too steep and time to walk so you can dismount easily and avoid a nasty tumble.

See you at the top!

Riding Downhill

One of mountain biking's greatest thrills is the descent. Like the skier, the accomplished mountain bike rider blends her or his technique with the terrain, making each hill a new challenge, dancing with nature. Many basic riding skills come into play as you roll down a winding dirt road or steep trail.

SAFETY TIP   As we consider the elements involved in a descent, the most important factor, as in all riding, is safety. Never attempt a radical maneuver without practice at the most basic level and never let your riding companions persuade you to ride faster than your own judgment and abilities allow.

Downhill skills mainly involve braking and weight distribution. You must be able to judge steepness, surface conditions, and proper clearance of obstacles.

Easy Brake Test

First, test your brakes on easy downhill terrain. This will familiarize you with your estimated stopping distance. Remember, the front brake is your most powerful; used improperly, it could launch you through the air! The best stop is through combined use of the front and rear brakes. On a descent, the rear brake is often used to control speed.

After you have developed a feeling for brake use and stopping power, you are ready to test yourself on a descent. Find an easy hill and ride it a few times, practicing your braking and weight distribution.

Braking efficiency and weight distribution are related; if your weight is back as you go down a hill, you will have more weight on both wheels and therefore more stopping power when you apply the brakes of both wheels.

Try this test at a slow speed and then faster after you gain confidence. While riding slowly down a hill, squeeze the front brake twice as hard as you squeeze the rear brake. Your body weight will immediately shift forward, possibly unweighting the rear wheel. This can cause a loss of control. When your rear wheel starts to jump or skid, let up on the front brake. Force your weight back by shifting your rear end over or behind the seat while standing on the pedals with your cranks in a horizontal position. This technique will help you slow down and greatly shorten your stopping distance. Practice this weight shift until you always feel in control.

David Epperson

Standing on the pedals and shifting your rear end over the seat will help you maintain control during descents.

Keep in mind that as you apply either brake the effect is to transfer your weight forward. Move your body weight back, sometimes even behind the seat. This will stop you faster and might save you from a spill.

Visualize yourself during this braking exercise. Your cranks are horizontal, your weight is evenly distributed, knees and elbows are bent to absorb any bumps, your head is up, eyes are looking ahead, and you are poised to steer in either direction and react quickly to any change in the terrain. An added advantage is that in this position your horizontal cranks have the greatest ground clearance over obstacles.

More Advanced Braking

After practicing basic braking on smooth, wide descents, you can test your skills on a tougher hill. For steep descents on either roads or single-track trails, more advanced techniques are needed.

On the steeps, the front brake is used with extreme care. Some good riders use it very little. You should learn to modulate your front brake, using it in conjunction with your rear brake and applying it for only a split second at a time to help control speed. Remember, your front wheel needs to keep rolling and steering, no matter how slowly, or you will definitely be on your way to a face-plant.

For really hairy descents, many advanced riders lower their seat height to allow them to get way back—with their stomachs near or actually on the saddle—to increase braking power.

On steep descents, keep your weight over the rear wheel and use the front brake sparingly.

■ MASTER DESCENTS

The new rider must always know how efficiently he or she can stop before attempting any descent. While your stopping power is controlled mainly by squeezing the brake levers for your front and rear brakes, body positioning is also important.

1. Prepare to descend by shifting up until you can maintain control of the pedals. If the descent is steep, lower your seat so you can shift your weight to the rear.
2. Squeeze the front and rear brakes. When your rear wheel starts to jump or skid, let up on the front brake. If the descent is very steep and fast, use the front brake only a split second at a time.
3. Force your weight back by shifting your rear end over or behind the seat when standing on the pedals with the cranks in a horizontal position.

Cornering

Cornering, especially at speed or on steeper downhills, often requires that you keep your outside pedal down. This is important for two reasons. It gives you the best pedal clearance on the inside of the turn and it counterbalances your bike and body. In some instances you will put some additional weight on the outside pedal as you enter the turn.

There are different ways to steer your bike through corners. You should attempt to lean the bike and your body by turning your hips into the corner; this is especially important for beginners who will quickly find this to be smoother and safer than turning the handlebars and risking a sudden spill. First lean the bike into the turn and then fine-tune the turn with body lean. If you lean your body too much in the early stages of a turn, the front wheel can wash out, and it will be difficult to tighten up a corner. It is easier to avoid a fall by not overcommitting the lean angle of your bike. Remember, if you enter a corner faster than you want and don't think you can make the turn, lean more. If the bike washes out, at

Always have your inside foot ready on the turn.

least you don't ride off an embankment or into the trees. Practice steering from the hips and leaning the bike more than your body.

You should always have your inside foot ready to catch yourself in case you lean too much on a turn. If you use toe clips, you might kick out or loosen them for a tough turn or descent. Always remember to let your bike roll through the apex of the turn—the tightest part, where you're leaning the most. It's easy to break loose if you brake in the turn. Reduce your chance of falling by braking hard before the turn, slowing to a comfortable speed, and then riding through the turn. If you don't let go of the brakes a little, you can't turn because there will likely be too much weight on the front wheel.

If the trail or road is either very loose or wet, be extra cautious with your front brake. This caution is needed because in loose dirt or gravel your rear wheel is likely to slide away from you. If it's wet, your brakes are more likely to grab.

■ LEARN TO TURN CORNERS SAFELY

Good preparation is the key to cornering.

1. Keep your outside pedal in a down position.
2. Shift your hips and lean your bike into the turn. Body lean can be used to fine-tune your turning.
3. Slow down early so your bike can roll through the apex of the turn.
4. If you use toe clips, kick out or loosen them when conditions are very difficult.

Handling Terrain Changes

Whenever you're riding off-road, you must be prepared to recognize and negotiate obstacles. These challenges may include ruts, logs, rocks, streams, curbs, or culverts.

Clearances are of most importance to the fast or downhill rider. You have to know what size obstacle can be crossed before your pedals or chainrings will hit. You can come to a very costly and abrupt stop if you misjudge. If you are unsure in approaching an obstacle, it is best to stop and check it out. Dismounting and rolling your bike over the object will help you determine clearance. Then, you can always go back and ride over it.

When crossing large ruts or culverts, never hit your front brake when dropping in. This can stop your front wheel and send you onward without

Riding the ruts in Durango, Colorado.

your bike. Besides the accident, major damage to your frame, fork, or wheel is a possibility. If you're not sure, again, walk it through the first time. Soon you will come to obstacles that appear impossible, but you will discover that you can ride them. But take your time.

When riding a particularly rutted road or trail, keep your vision focused well ahead of you. Ruts can be very tricky; you may need to roll in or out at an opportune time to avoid major drop-offs or unpassable sections. Sometimes it's best to ride in the ruts; sometimes it's better to skirt the ruts. Sometimes you get in a rut and can't get out.

Avoid rocks when possible. In rough, rocky sections, ride with weight evenly distributed. Look for the least rock-strewn line. Sharp rocks cause more flat tires on mountain bikes than perhaps any other obstacle.

Watch for deep sand. It can stop you dead in your tracks. Stay seated and let the bike roll through a sandy section. Try to ride the more packed section or skirt the sandy area altogether for better traction. (Hint: Riding in sandy, saltwater areas can cause corrosion to your equipment, so wash your bike afterward.)

In summary, let safety be your guide as you roll down hills and through the many challenges in terrain. The more you ride, the more confidence you will gain. While descending, shift up in anticipation of the hill ahead, use your brakes in combination, and keep your body weight back. Always be aware of possible oncoming traffic. Never ride faster than you feel is safe, and never let your friends dictate the pace.

See you at the bottom!

David Epperson

Riding on packed sand makes for easier pedaling.

Crossing Water

Water crossings can be an exciting test of skill, determination, and judgment, plus they can be very refreshing during a hot ride. But always use caution. As you approach a creek bed, look for the shallowest area. To keep your feet dry, keep your cranks horizontal. This, of course, is not always possible—sometimes you'll have to pedal through the crossing and it may be deeper than pedal level.

Carry good momentum into the stream but always be on the lookout for large rocks or other submerged obstacles that could impede your progress. If you need to pedal, stay seated for better traction and stability.

On your stream approach, be sure to shift to a smaller gear—if you can't coast through, at least you'll be in a lower gear and ready to pedal so you won't bog down in midstream. If you cannot see the bottom because of muddy water, take extra care or avoid entirely if possible.

Did you make it across? Good job. Now you can watch your friends to see whether they pedal or paddle.

David Epperson

Getting across water is a fun challenge.

■ CROSS WATER SKILLFULLY

1. Look for the shallowest area of water.
2. Keep your cranks horizontal if you can coast through the water.
3. Shift to a lower gear if you can't coast through the water.
4. Stay seated for good traction and stability.

Carrying Your Bike

When it is time to dismount and carry your bike, try this safe and easy carrying technique. Standing on the left of your bike (you don't want to get greasy from your chain or chainrings), put your right arm through the frame, reach around, grab the handlebar and pull it toward you.

The bike will rest on your right shoulder where the top tube and the seat tube meet. Or you can simply hoist your bike onto your right shoulder balancing it with your right hand under the top tube.

David Epperson

When it's impossible to keep riding, the shoulder carry is an effective way to get your bike over obstacles.

The shoulder carry is a relatively comfortable carrying method for people of all shapes and sizes. It is more difficult to carry a traditional women's-style bike; this is one reason why many women ride men's models.

Always keep your left hand free for balance. If you carry your bike a great deal, get a portage strap or add padding so your load will be more comfortable on your shoulder.

Outdoor Awareness and Trail Etiquette

The mountain bike allows more people than ever before to enjoy scenic outdoor and wilderness areas. Ridden carefully, a mountain bike will leave few imprints on pristine wilderness areas. Like the backpacker who leaves only footprints, the aware mountain bike rider leaves nothing more than a tire track.

Outdoor awareness, courtesy, and safe riding practices are essential if mountain bike riders hope to continue to share trails with other outdoor enthusiasts. Mountain biking's continued growth and reputation will be determined in large part by the image projected by today's riders. Unsafe, selfish use of trails, more than anything else, will spoil public land use and limit access for future generations of mountain bike riders.

Already, trails in some heavily used areas have been closed to mountain bike riders. Some of the closures are due to rude behavior and lack of respect on the part of unthinking riders. On the positive side, mountain bike groups have opened trails after demonstrating commitment to trail sharing and environmental awareness. Many mountain bike clubs are building and maintaining trails as community service projects.

Although mountain bikes are quiet, low-impact vehicles, they can be used in a manner threatening to other trail users. We must respect the

David Epperson

Respectfully yielding the right of way to other trail users in the San Juan Mountains of Colorado.

rights of hikers, horseback riders, and nature lovers. Each type of use has its place. If you're riding through a scenic mountain area frequented by bird-watchers or other wildlife observers, it is obviously best to ride slowly and quietly. A friendly, low-volume bell on your handlebar can be used to signal your approach in a quiet manner. Save your fast action for a place where others won't be bothered. We must be careful not to disturb wildlife in our riding areas. Since mountain bikers are among the newest additions to the list of wilderness users, we must be careful to show that we are good neighbors, that we are safe and responsible riders.

Many of us think that mountain bikes can be less damaging to the environment than horses. They can bring wilderness enjoyment to more people and, as a result, help build more support for resource conservation efforts. Although there have been a few complaints about mountain bike damage to trail systems, there is no scientific proof that mountain bikers cause any more environmental damage than other trail users.

When it comes to outdoor awareness, the message should be clear to all mountain bikers: Ride safely, courteously, and responsibly. Otherwise, all mountain bikers may pay the price of an irresponsible few.

EARTH WATCH

Responsible mountain bikers . . .

. . . don't trespass.

. . . don't litter.

. . . don't ride through wet meadows.

. . . ride at safe speeds.

. . . respect private property.

IMBA RULES OF THE TRAIL

1. Ride on open trails only. Respect trail and road closures (ask if you're not sure), avoid possible trespass on private land, obtain permits and authorization as may be required. Federal and state wilderness areas are closed to cycling.
2. Leave no trace. Be sensitive to the dirt beneath you. Even on open trails, you should not ride under conditions where you will leave evidence of your passing, such as on certain soils shortly after a rain. Observe the different types of soils and trail construction; practice low-impact cycling. This also means staying on the trail and not creating any new ones. Be sure to pack out at least as much as you pack in.
3. Control your bicycle. Inattention for even a second can cause problems. Obey all speed laws.
4. Always yield the trail. Make known your approach well in advance. A friendly greeting (or a bell) is considerate and works well; don't startle others. Show your respect when passing others by slowing to a walk or even stopping. Anticipate that other trail users may be around corners or in blind spots.
5. Never spook animals. All animals are startled by an unannounced approach, a sudden movement, or a loud noise. This can be dangerous for you, for others, and for the animals. Give animals

extra room and time to adjust to you. When passing horses, use special care and follow the rider's directions (as if you're uncertain). Running cattle and disturbing wild animals is a serious offense. Leave gates as you found them, or as marked.

6. Plan ahead. Know your equipment, your ability, and the area in which you are riding—and prepare accordingly. Be self-sufficient at all times. Wear a helmet, keep your machine in good condition, and carry necessary supplies for changes in weather or other conditions. A well-executed trip is a satisfaction to you and not a burden or offense to others.

4

HEALTHY AND SAFE MOUNTAIN BIKING

Few outdoor pursuits compare with mountain biking to combine adventure, fun, and fitness. No matter where you live or how you ride, you can increase your fitness level, feel better about yourself, and add new vigor to your life.

Each time you hop on your bike, you will be able to seek out new challenges to your riding abilities and at the same time improve your strength, flexibility, and cardiorespiratory system.

Mountain biking is the sport for many of us who want to improve our physical condition but find repetitive indoor exercises to be tedious. Pumping iron or pedaling a stationary bicycle might make us stronger, but sweating in a gym can't match the excitement of blue sky, fresh air, and the great outdoors.

As we ride mountain bikes, we are able to let the adventuresome spirit inside of us escape and come out to play. At the same time we can develop a youthful vitality, possibly adding years to our lives through increased strength, endurance, and cardiorespiratory fitness.

And because we are able to explore some very beautiful places, mountain biking also allows peace of mind and mental relaxation—stress reduction, if you prefer. During your rides you may work out personal and family issues and develop creative new solutions to business or career challenges you have been thinking about.

Contemplating new horizons—one of the rewards of mountain biking.

How Ready Is Your Body?

You don't need to be in top physical shape to take up mountain biking. Cycling is an activity that nearly everyone can pursue, regardless of age. If you enjoy a brisk walk, you will enjoy a brisk ride. Certainly if you do ride your mountain bike regularly, you will improve your physical condition, especially your heart and lung capacity.

One of the most appealing aspects of cycling is that it's gentle on the body—a nonimpact form of exercise. It is perhaps one of the most exciting activities that does not put heavy impacts on the athlete's knees, ankles, or back. Of course, cycling can be extremely demanding, depending on conditions and terrain. But in cycling you are much less likely than in other activities to be sore or unable to exercise for days afterward because of aching muscles or joints. This is an important attraction for many people who must limit jarring exercise because of age or injury.

Another attraction of cycling is that each rider may choose his or her own level of participation and energy output. This is one of the reasons cycling, particularly mountain biking, is gaining converts from other activities such as running, tennis, and skiing. The low risk of injury and high fitness benefit are tough to match.

Mountain biking provides a good workout, and each rider can set her own pace.

Before taking up mountain biking, or any other active pursuit, you should get approval from your personal physician. This is most important for middle-aged and older people who want to adopt a more active lifestyle. If you want to enjoy the activity as well as receive its health benefits, it's always wise to know your starting point.

If you've ever ridden a bike, you can ride a mountain bike. If you have doubts about your physical condition or endurance level, cycling is good because you can take it easy the first time out and then increase time and distance at your own pace.

Find an initial off-road adventure that is not too hilly or tough to ride. The terrain you choose will definitely determine your enjoyment level. First-timers should seek out graded or groomed trails or dirt roads. If the route can be traveled by a motor vehicle, it is probably not overly steep. The next step up would typically be a fire road or double-track trail. Survey the horizon, estimate elevations, and decide whether you're ready for something steeper. The most difficult and technically demanding riding will be found on single-track trails and in the more mountainous areas. Use extreme caution when entering expert terrain for the first time. Advanced riding skills, balance, and top physical conditioning are recommended.

Your community bike shop can direct you to the nearby trails best suited to your physical condition and riding ability.

Improving Your Mountain Biking Fitness

Although you can enjoy a first moderate outing without a high level of physical fitness, the fitter you are, the more you'll be able to enjoy mountain biking. As your flexibility, strength, and cardiorespiratory fitness increase, you'll be able to ride longer, ride farther, and handle tougher terrains.

Basic Stretching Guidelines and Exercises for Cyclists

It is always a good idea to stretch your muscles before and after riding. Bob and Jean Anderson, authors of *Stretching* recommend these guidelines and stretches for bikers.[1]

Stretching should be done slowly without bouncing. Stretch to where you feel a slight, easy stretch. Hold this feeling for 5 to 30 seconds. Hold only stretch tensions that feel good to you. The key to stretching is to be relaxed while you concentrate on the area being stretched. Your breathing should be slow, deep, and rhythmical. Don't worry about how far you can stretch. Stretch relaxed, and limberness will become just one of the many by-products of regular stretching.

---

[1]*Note.* Text excerpted from *Cycling Stretches,* © 1992 (22-1/2'' × 34'' poster) by Bob and Jean Anderson. Reprinted by permission. For a free catalog, write to Stretching, Inc., P.O. Box 767, Palmer Lake, CO 80133, or call 1-800-333-1307.

CALF STRETCH   Stand a little way from a solid support and lean on it with your forearms, your head resting on your hands. Bend one leg and place your foot on the ground in front of you leaving the other leg straight behind you. Slowly move your hips forward until you feel a stretch in the calf of your straight leg. Be sure to keep the heel of the foot of the straight leg on the ground and your toes pointed straight ahead. Hold an easy stretch for 30 seconds. Do not bounce. Stretch both legs.

CALF STRETCH

HAMSTRING AND LOWER BACK STRETCH   Sit on the floor and straighten your right leg. Put the sole of your left foot next to the inside of your straightened leg. Lean slightly forward from the hips and stretch the hamstrings of your right leg. Find an easy stretch and relax. If you can't touch your toes comfortably, hook a towel around your foot to help you stretch. Hold for 30 seconds. Do not lock your knee. Your right quadriceps should be soft and relaxed during the stretch. Keep your right foot upright with the ankle and toes relaxed. Repeat the stretch with your left leg.

HAMSTRING AND LOWER BACK STRETCH

ARMS, SHOULDERS, AND UPPER BACK STRETCH   Hold on to your bike. With your hands shoulder-width apart on this support, relax, keeping your arms straight and your chest moving downward and your feet remaining directly under your hips. Keep your knees slightly bent. Hold this stretch 30 seconds. Remember to always bend your knees when coming out of this stretch.

ARMS, SHOULDERS, AND UPPER BACK STRETCH

QUADRICEPS AND KNEE STRETCH While standing, grab the top of your right foot (from inside of foot) with your left hand and gently pull, moving your heel toward your buttocks. The knee bends at a natural angle in this position and creates a good stretch in the knee and quads. Hold for 30 seconds. Do both legs.

QUADRICEPS AND KNEE STRETCH

ACHILLES TENDONS, GROIN, LOWER BACK, AND HIPS STRETCH

With your feet shoulder-width apart and pointed out to about a 15-degree angle, heels on the ground, bend your knees and squat. If you have trouble staying in this position, hold on to something for support. Hold the stretch for 30 seconds. Be careful if you have had any knee problems. If pain is present, discontinue this stretch.

ACHILLES TENDONS, GROIN, LOWER BACK, AND HIPS STRETCH

Warming Up and Cooling Down

The first 10 to 20 minutes of riding is the warm-up phase. The warm-up should be a prelude to every ride. Pace yourself and take some time reaching your fastest pace.

At the end of each ride comes the cool-down—10 to 15 minutes of reduced energy output. The warm-up will help prevent injuries and the cool-down will help speed your recovery time from the ride. The warm-up and cool-down should be a regular beginning and end to your rides.

Cardiorespiratory Fitness

Cardiorespiratory fitness is the most important physical benefit you can achieve from mountain biking. The higher your cardiorespiratory fitness, the more you will be able to enjoy your mountain bike.

One way to get an idea of your level of cardiorespiratory fitness is to listen to your body as you ride. If you become winded or can't carry on a conversation with your fellow riders, you're probably riding too hard. Slow down and look for a comfortable rhythm.

Another way to check your cardiorespiratory fitness is to monitor your heart rate. And checking your pulse before, during, and after your rides will allow you to chart progress. After a few weeks or months of riding you will find marked improvement, especially in your heart recovery rate after a spurt of effort.

You can use the gears on your mountain bike as a factor in determining how much energy you expend during a ride. Depending on the surface you're riding on, you might try a pedal cadence in the range of 75 revolutions per minute. This rate is generally effective for improving cardiorespiratory fitness. Always try to turn the pedals with a fluid motion and to develop a feeling for applying pressure throughout the pedal stroke.

Getting Your Muscles Ready for Riding

Regular riding will allow you to gradually improve your muscular strength, and as your strength increases you'll be able to ride farther, higher, and longer. Take it easy at first. Don't try to ride 10 miles (16 km) of tough trails your first time out. Let your body be your guide to how hard you push yourself. If you want some added help in improving your muscular strength so you can enjoy those steeper hills and rougher trails, try some resistance training. We explain a few exercises, which use only your body weight to provide the resistance, that will strengthen your whole body. Perhaps surprisingly, your upper body strength has a big effect on your hill-climbing ability.

USE HEART RATE TO GAUGE
CARDIORESPIRATORY FITNESS

Specialists in sports medicine generally agree that to receive benefits from aerobic exercise such as cycling, you must work hard enough to get your heart pumping at 60 percent to 85 percent of your maximum heart rate and maintain this pace for 20 minutes to 30 minutes per workout. Here's how to determine your target heart rate range and how to check your pulse:

Finding Your Target Heart Rate Range

1. Subtract your age from 220 to calculate your approximate maximum heart rate.
2. Multiply your approximate maximum heart rate by 0.6 to find your lower heart rate target.
3. Multiply your approximate maximum heart rate by 0.85 to find your upper heart rate target.*

To get health benefits, your heart rate during aerobic exercise should fall between the upper and lower limits you just calculated.

Determining Your Heart Rate

1. Locate your pulse by pressing gently with your index and middle fingers at the base of your wrist or at the side of your neck near the Adam's apple.
2. Count the number of beats you feel in 15 seconds.
3. Multiply your 15-second count by 4 to determine your heart rate in beats per minute.

*You should talk with your doctor about this range if you take heart or blood pressure medicine. The medication may dictate that you use a lower heart rate range.

Start out trying to do 3 sets of 10 repetitions of each exercise. If you can't do that many, do what you can and increase the number of reps or sets as you feel you're ready.

DIPS You'll need two sturdy chairs with seats the same height for this exercise. Place them, seats facing each other, about 4 or 5 feet (1.2-1.5 m) apart (you may need to adjust this distance depending on your height). Place your hands on the edge of one chair seat, and your feet on the seat of the second chair. Lower yourself slowly, then straighten your elbows completely to lift yourself.

DIPS

PARTIAL SIT-UP Lie on your back on the floor with your knees bent, feet flat on the floor, and arms crossed over your chest. Press your lower back against the floor. Raise your shoulder blades off the floor by curling your head and shoulders up and forward until you can touch your knees with your hands. Hold this position for 2 or 3 seconds, then return your shoulders and head to the floor.

PARTIAL SIT-UP

PUSH-UPS Lie on your stomach with your palms flat on the floor about shoulder-width apart and your toes pointing down. Straighten your arms to lift your body, being sure to keep your back straight. You should be looking at the floor slightly in front of your hands. Keep your back straight, and lower your body by bending at the elbows until your chest touches the floor.

You can make this exercise easier by placing your knees on the floor instead of your toes. You can make the exercise harder by moving your hands wider apart.

PUSH-UPS

SQUAT Stand with your feet flat on the floor about shoulder-width apart and your toes pointing straight forward. Bend at the knees and hips until your thighs are parallel to the floor, making sure your feet stay flat and your head stays upright. Putting your arms straight out in front of you as you bend may make balancing easier. Straighten your knees and hips to return to the starting position.

SQUAT

CALF RAISES   Stand up straight with your feet on the floor and your arms at your sides. Rise onto your toes as far as you can, then slowly lower yourself.

To make this exercise harder, you can stand on the edge of a step (only your toes are on the step). Be sure to hold on to the handrail if you do this. You can also do this exercise on a step using only one leg at a time.

CALF RAISES

Energy Tips

You'll ride better and stronger if your body is properly fueled for the outing. This goes for both solid and liquid fuel.

Learn to recognize the benefits of simple and complex carbohydrates, the best source of energy for mountain biking or any other prolonged physical exercise. Look for fiber, grains, and vegetables when fueling up. Avoid large quantities of fats and proteins before a ride; they will serve only to slow you down in digestion time and energy output.

It's important to keep well hydrated when riding. Many riders will use 12 to 16 ounces (.35 to .47 liters) of water per hour, even in cooler conditions. It's a good idea to carry two water bottles on longer rides—with water in one and a premixed energy drink in the other. This combination will help keep you from dehydrating and losing energy. Find a carbo drink that pleases your taste buds and be sure to mix it properly. Too concentrated a mixture is hard to digest and may cause higher blood sugar and stomach upset.

Always bring along something solid to munch if you're planning to ride for more than an hour.

Always carry plenty of liquids with you on your rides.

Maintaining Your Bike for Safe Riding

A well-maintained mountain bike is essential to safe and worry-free riding. A poorly adjusted brake, loose connection, or other equipment failure can cause accident or injury.

You do not have to be mechanically inclined; mountain bikes are easy to understand and low in maintenance. You should learn the basics of cable adjustments and be prepared to repair a flat tire in off-road situations.

Barrel Cable Adjustments

It is not uncommon for new brake and shifter cables to stretch and need adjustment after a few weeks or months of riding. If you are on the trail and your brake levers suddenly squeeze all the way to your handlebar, you will definitely want to know how to adjust them.

Take a moment to inspect the barrel cable adjustments on your hand brake levers and shifters and ask for an adjustment demonstration at your

On-the-trail maintenance.

bike shop. Cables are easily adjusted on most newer bikes; many can be adjusted as you ride, without even stopping.

Lubrication

Lubrication should be applied lightly and at regular intervals to the chain and all pivot points on the derailleurs and shifting levers. Try to use a lube designed for mountain bikes. These lubes are designed to work better in the wetter and dirtier conditions found in off-road riding. If you ride in moderately wet conditions, you should have a shop repack your hubs, bottom bracket, and headset every year or two, unless you own a bike with sealed bearings that can't be serviced. This will increase the life of your bike dramatically. Have your bike shop advise you on what service is needed for sealed bearings.

Tools You May Need

A compact set of Allen wrenches and a small crescent wrench will allow you to work with just about every fitting on your bike.

Carrying a chain tool with extra chain pins will allow you to make on-trail chain repairs. A spoke wrench may be needed on rare occasions to tighten or loosen wheel spokes.

Carry a few zip ties. They can be used like baling wire for emergency repairs.

■ FIX A FLAT TIRE

Your saddle pack repair kit should include a spare inner tube, a patch kit, duct tape, and tire levers. You should also carry a pump.

If you have a flat tire, pull over and be sure you are out of the way of other cyclists or vehicles before starting the repairs.

1. Undo the yoke to the brake, undo the wheel's quick release, and remove the wheel. If it is a rear tire, shift to the smallest cog first so the wheel will slide out easier.
2. Visually inspect the tire for the cause of the flat. If the tire is severely damaged, it may not be fixable.
3. To repair, brace the wheel between your legs, with the valve at the bottom. At the top, insert the tire levers under the tire bead, about 6 inches (15 cm) apart. Use the levers individually to pry a 6-inch (15-cm) section of tire off the rim. Now remove the tire from one side of the rim and remove the tube.
4. Run your finger carefully around the inside of the tire to check for a protruding object. Watch for sharp objects such as thorns, nails, or glass. Remove the object. If your tread or sidewall is cut or gashed, repair from the inside using duct tape.
5. If you're patching a tube, find the hole, buff around the hole with your kit's sandpaper, partially inflate, add glue, let dry for a few minutes, then press on the patch.
6. Partially inflate your spare or repaired tube to give it shape. Insert the valve in the rim and fit the tube into the tire. Then starting at the valve, work the bead back on the rim. Thumb pressure usually works. You may have to use tire levers for the last 6 to 8 inches (15 to 20 cm). Be careful that you don't puncture the tube.
7. Fully inflate the tire with your pump, checking to see that the tire is seated evenly. Put the wheel back on, fasten the quick release, and reattach the brake yoke piece.

Congratulations. You have just solved mountain biking's most common problem!

Cautions for Safe Riding

As you develop your mountain biking skills, you will also develop more confidence in your abilities. But don't become overconfident. Just when you feel you can handle every situation, a new one arises. Always ride

WHEN YOUR CHAIN COMES OFF

Chain derailment is a problem most mountain bikers will have to face: Due to a quick or powerful shift, a bump, or a pedal hesitation, the bike chain jumps off the chainrings. The problem usually occurs on the large front chainrings but can occur on the rear freewheel. In either case, stop your bike immediately. Make sure you have shifted to the smallest chainring, and then gently pull part of the chain back onto the ring. Lift the rear wheel slightly, and turn the pedals slowly by hand until the chain slips completely back into position.

If the chain jumps inside the bigger ring in the rear, there is a greater chance of a jam (and of spoke damage). Gently pull and massage the chain to remove it if it has become wedged between the freewheel and the spokes.

safely, alertly, and within your comfort zone. Above all, never leave your helmet and other safety equipment at home.

Ride with a companion whenever possible; if you're riding alone always make sure someone knows where you're going and what time you expect to return.

There are untold factors that can cause a cycling accident and, unfortunately, the rider cannot control or predict every possibility. By being vigilant, prepared, and properly equipped, the rider can greatly reduce the chance for accident or injury.

Remember, good judgment is your most important tool.

SAFETY TIP It's a good idea to carry some money and personal identification on your person or in your seat pack. Paper money can be used for an emergency inside-the-tire patch and, of course, a little cash never hurts when thirst or hunger sets in. Carrying an ID is important in case an accident should occur. As an alternative, write your name, address, and phone number on the inside of your helmet.

PRERIDE SAFETY CHECKS

Smart cyclists check their bikes as well as their personal safety gear before each ride.

Feel your tires for air pressure. Check the quick releases on your front and rear wheels (this is especially important for riders who remove wheels regularly to transport the bike). Be sure your brakes are working. A common error is to take off a wheel and forget to reattach the brake cable and yoke after putting the wheel back on. Always check your brakes before pedaling off. Take a look to see that your brake pads are securely hitting the rims on each side. Spin the front and rear wheels and apply the brakes. Make sure the pads are making proper contact when braking.

Make sure your helmet is buckled securely around your chin. Wear protective glasses and gloves.

5

THE BEST PLACES TO MOUNTAIN BIKE

The wonder of mountain biking lies in the go-anywhere nature of the activity. No matter where you live—in the city, in the country, in the hills, or on the flat—you can find a place to have fun on your mountain bike. You can explore the neighborhoods and backroads of your own community or you can travel to exotic places and experience some of the world's finest mountain biking trails.

In recent years, there has been a dramatic increase in the number of tour companies that offer complete, preplanned cycling vacations. Many established companies that entered the business by offering road bike tours are now specializing in off-road, fat-tire tours and are finding new markets for their services.

Mountain biking has become a popular summertime activity at ski resort communities in the U.S. and abroad. Instead of closing down in the summer, ski lifts are carrying mountain bikers to mountain tops. Shedding their winter coats, ski runs become bike trails. Resort operators see mountain biking as a natural extension of their business: an environmentally conscious way to generate needed revenues at a time of year when their lodges and lifts were once quiet. Some resorts have opened complete mountain bike centers with instructional programs, rentals, marked trails, obstacle courses, mountain bike polo, and other organized activities.

Many ski resorts become mountain biking meccas during the summer months.

Wherever your riding takes you, remember to respect nature and don't trespass on private property. Make sure mountain bikes are allowed on the trail you want to ride. Mountain biking is allowed on most public land in the United States and open trail access is available in many other countries, but there are some restrictions and closed trails. For example, off-road riding is prohibited in U.S. national parks, although this policy can and should change, subject to certain limitations.

Finding the Best Local Rides

You'll quickly discover local roads and trails best suited to your riding tastes. To find new options, you might check with parks and forestry offices. More of these governmental units are developing trails and publishing trail maps.

Public parks can be well suited for novice and family riders. Trails are frequently gentle and well marked, trail maps are often available, and there are usually other riders in the area, an advantage if an emergency should occur.

Topographical (topo) maps that provide detailed elevation and distance information about specific areas are available in bike shops, camping and outdoor outlets, and from local printing and map or blueprint stores. (In the United States, the U.S. Geological Service produces excellent topo maps.) Local bike shops will often have wall maps or flyers describing favorite local rides.

Residents of smaller towns often find nice riding on dirt roads that wind into the surrounding countryside. Urban cyclists may have to travel a little farther before pedaling peacefully into the hills.

A peaceful country ride can provide a refreshing change of scenery for city dwellers.

If you have a shortage of trails in or near your community, be patient; they're coming. Local cities, counties, recreation commissions, bike clubs, and trails councils have recognized the need for more nonmotorized trails and many civic efforts are underway in this direction. Better yet, pitch in and help. Scout out trail locations, volunteer, and help make mountain biking more accessible in your area.

Day Trips and Weekends

After you've mastered the local trail loops, you'll be looking for new challenges. Check out trail or topographical maps of your nearest mountain recreation areas. Plan a day or weekend trip to an area that offers a pleasant and challenging ride, or sign up for a club ride.

Contact the local bike shops for firsthand trail information. Chambers of commerce, resort associations, and parks departments also can be of help. Getting the inside scoop from the locals always makes for a better ride. Don't be afraid to ask how steep or technical the trails are. Your ride should match your skill and fitness levels.

In some of the more popular mountain biking areas in California, Colorado, and other U.S. states, there has been a proliferation in recent years of local bike trail guides. These handy and informative booklets contain a wealth of local trail details and are usually well worth the investment of a few dollars per copy. There's no trail guide for your region? Write one.

Transporting Your Bike

Most mountain bikers transport their bikes in or on their personal vehicles. For greater distances, airplane and train bicycle transport is becoming more accepted.

Today's modern mountain bikes are easily disassembled, so many riders carry their bikes inside their vehicles. In many cases, all you have to do is remove a quick release front wheel and put your bike in the trunk or behind the seat in a station wagon or sport utility vehicle. With smaller vehicles, you may also have to remove the rear wheel. Advantages of carrying your bike inside include less chance of theft and less weather exposure.

Roof racks are popular these days. The roof rack has virtually been reinvented in recent years by companies such as Thule and Yakima. These new multipurpose racks have attachments for bikes as well as boards, kayaks, canoes, and skis. Expect to pay about $300 to $400 for a high-quality roof rack with bike attachments and locks. Fully loaded roof racks can carry up to six bikes, but four is a more comfortable number. Never drive into your garage with your roof rack loaded! This can cause serious damage to bike, vehicle, and home. And always make sure your rack and bikes are securely attached. You don't want to lose your load as you travel.

David Epperson

Roof racks help you get your bike to new places to ride.

Rear racks mount on the rear or trunk deck of your vehicle. They are small and convenient and most are easy to put on and take off. Most have a two- or three-bike carrying capacity. One drawback with most rear-mount racks is that they prevent access to trunk or rear-end doors or windows. A proper fit is imperative. Rear-mount racks can shift and vibrate, causing scuffing and scratching to your vehicle's paint. Always look for well-made, padded feet on a rear rack. Expect to pay $40 to $50 for low-end rear-mount racks and up to $100 or $120 for the best models.

If you drive a pickup, special bed racks allow you to secure your bikes so they don't bounce around.

Air transport can be expensive, but with more people taking cycling vacations and more businesspeople packing their bikes, air travel with bikes is becoming accepted. Normally you will pay a $40 to $60 excess baggage charge for your bike. Bike-friendly airlines will throw in a bike box for the price.

Bike shops are often prepared to pack your bike in a transport box for $20 or $25. Find a shop that offers this service, especially if you have an expensive bike. See how the bike is packed and next time try it yourself.

For packing, you must loosen the stem and turn or remove the handlebar. The front wheel and the pedals must also be removed.

Boxes work well, but if you and your bike are frequent travel companions, consider purchasing a soft- or hard-shell bike transport bag. They are expensive, $300 and up, but worth the investment in convenience and bicycle protection.

In most cases, train transport is easy and convenient. Your bike will be stowed in a baggage car without charge or special packaging.

AT A GLANCE: BIKE CARRIERS

Roof Racks

Advantages: Carries more. Frees trunk. Can carry other equipment.

Disadvantages: Expensive. Hard to reach and load. Driver must be on the lookout for overhead obstacles.

Rear Racks

Advantages: Inexpensive. Mounting rack is easy. Mounting bikes is easy. Collapsible.

Disadvantages: Prevents access to trunk. Carries only two or three bikes. Bikes and vehicles are more easily scratched and damaged.

Planning a Ride

As you look over maps and other literature to select a ride, try to look for new challenges but don't pick a ride that's too radical. Your route should be at least 90 percent ridable—a little uphill walking and pushing is all right to get to an exciting descent, but too much walking becomes tiresome.

When you're starting out, try to find off-road rides in the 5- to 15-mile (8- to 24-km) range. Keep in mind that it may take an hour or more to go 5 or 6 miles (8 or 10 km) in rugged terrain. Real trail conditions can be quite different from the way they appear on a map. For example, highly trained mountain bike racers who compete in extremely rugged conditions often average only 11 to 12 mph (18 to 19 kph). Plan plenty of time and don't be caught in unfamiliar areas after the sun goes down.

Ride with another person whenever possible because accidents are always a possibility, especially when you're exploring new turf. Be particularly careful when you're on a trail for the first time. The unexpected hazards can be many. If you do ride alone, make it a habit to tell someone what route you are following and when you will return.

Read your maps closely, and check elevation changes and total distance. When venturing more than walking distance from civilization, always plan your provisions; carry extra fluids, energy bars, and rain gear. A compass comes in handy on these rides and your cycle computer becomes more valuable.

Like the trappers, scouts, and explorers of frontier days, attune yourself with nature and your surroundings. Learn to follow tracks. That fat-tire track on the trail could lead to a very special ride.

Also remember that mountain bike riders must be especially careful not to trespass on private property. It's important for us to observe property rights and obey the law so that we don't create problems for other mountain bikers and the public image of mountain biking.

Riding the Ski Resorts

Ski areas have quickly and naturally become some of the most popular mountain bike gathering places. In the United States alone, close to 100 ski resorts transform themselves into mountain bike parks in what once was their off-season. At first the resorts were the domain of radical mountain bike kamikazes careening wildly down the slopes, but today they cater strongly to novices and families.

Prepare to pay $10 to $20 a day to ride up ski lifts with your bike and cruise down the resorts' trails. Some areas do not operate their lifts in the summer but still allow trail riding, usually with purchase of a trail pass. Cross-country ski areas often open their trails to mountain biking during the warm months. They also require a trail pass in most cases.

Nearly every resort with a mountain biking program offers bike and helmet rentals, so don't worry if a member of your group is short on equipment. Resort rentals are usually solid, durable, and well maintained.

Be sure to stay on marked trails. Many of the resorts have trail maps that show degree of trail difficulty. Often the resort's ski trail map will suffice. Recognize the standard trail marker signs: green for easiest, blue for more difficult, and black for most difficult. You probably won't want to bicycle down a double black diamond ski run!

Many resorts offer package mountain bike weekends or vacations, with a range of accommodations and dining choices. Or you may choose to stay at a nearby campground or bed and breakfast inn.

Remember, mountain weather is changeable so when heading to ski country, pack accordingly. Many resorts are at higher elevations so be sure to acclimatize yourself to avoid high altitude fatigue. Protect yourself against sunburn.

Mountain Bike Vacations

When you're ready to make tracks to the world's best mountain biking, you can do it on your own or use the services of a mountain bike tour operator.

By joining a tour, all the details are taken care of, leaving you to enjoy the ride. Support vehicles carry your gear, and meals and activities are provided at inns or camps along the trail. Experienced guides explain the geology, history, and culture of the area and offer tips to improve your riding techniques.

On the other hand, when traveling on your own, with family or friends, your schedule can be looser, you can set your own itinerary and pace, and you can change your plans on a whim. Stay where you wish by night and ride by day.

Biking vacations make for fun family getaways.

Cost, of course, may be your first consideration on how to travel. Is a tour experience worth the price or should you go it alone? A 5-day tour with premium accommodations and three meals a day may cost $850 to $1,100, or about $170 to more than $200 per day. A 5-day tour with campground accommodations will cost less, perhaps $600 to $700 for a 5-day trip.

If you will be riding for several days or a week, in addition to your camp gear and provisions, take an extra tire, a few tubes, a patch kit, an extra gear and brake cable, and basic tools, including crescent and Allen wrenches.

If you're traveling long distances for your tour, you may wish to rent a mountain bike instead of bringing your own. Rental of a high-quality bike adds about $100 to $120 to the 5-day tour price but may eliminate transportation costs and headaches. To ensure more comfortable riding, some riders bring their own bike seat and mount it on the rental bike.

Riders who choose self-guided tours to premium areas can expect to pay in the range of $80 to $100 per day for food and lodging. Remember, if you're touring on your own, you may need to purchase panniers and other gear, and this will add to the cost of your mountain bike vacation.

If you're visiting a premium destination, do you want to enjoy the area to its fullest? Maybe you should join a group for your first visit and return another time to explore the area with family or friends.

Most tours are geared toward the reasonably fit person, perhaps too slow for the highly tuned cyclist or too tough for the practiced couch potato. Good tours will match abilities or split groups and then rendezvous later in the day. Be prepared and in shape for a bike tour. You won't have an enjoyable ride if you can't keep up.

United States Getaways

Some of mountain biking's most notable destinations have emerged from early mountain bike festivals. First the racers came. Recreational riders, families, and tour companies weren't far behind.

In the United States, Crested Butte and Durango, Colorado; Moab, Utah; Mammoth Mountain and Big Bear Lake, California; Chequamegon, Wisconsin; Jim Thorpe, Pennsylvania; and Slaty Fork, West Virginia are popular and have gained widespread publicity through annual festivals. For a real glimpse into the world of mountain biking, a visit to one of these festivals should be on your vacation calendar.

Although it is a fast-growing sport and lifestyle, mountain biking has yet to have a significant effect on travel and leisure publishing. However, travel articles on mountain biking are beginning to appear more regularly and more attention is expected as the activity grows and matures, embracing new generations of travelers.

Listed here are just a few of the more recognized mountain bike centers. As you travel around your region, state, nation, or the globe enjoying mountain biking, you will undoubtedly discover other locations that deserve mention in future editions.

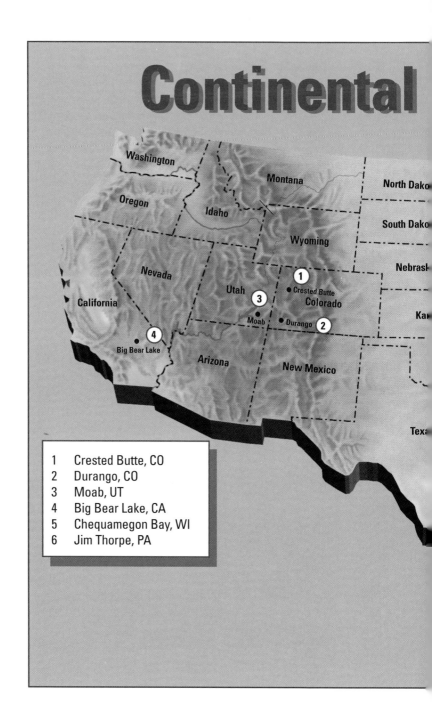

Continental

1   Crested Butte, CO
2   Durango, CO
3   Moab, UT
4   Big Bear Lake, CA
5   Chequamegon Bay, WI
6   Jim Thorpe, PA

nited States

Maine

VT

NH

Minnesota

Chequamegon Bay

Wisconsin

Michigan

New York

Mass.

Conn.

RI

Iowa

Pennsylvania

NJ

Illinois

Indiana

Ohio

West Virginia

MD

Delaware

Missouri

Kentucky

Virginia

Jim Thorpe

Arkansas

Tennessee

North Carolina

South Carolina

Louisiana

Alabama

Georgia

Mississippi

Florida

N

5

6

A YEAR-ROUND ACTIVITY

Cycling is no longer just a warm-weather sport. Modern equipment and all-weather apparel allow mountain bikers to ride comfortably year-round, and each season of the year has its own special rewards.

Die-hard riders can be seen pedaling around snow-covered mountain resort areas in midwinter, with studded tires on their bicycles. Some resorts have even held downhill mountain bike races on snowy courses.

David Epperson

My favorite riding season is autumn. The changing tones of the landscape, the cooler temperatures, and the end of season solitude make this a special time of year.

Dried leaves crunch and fly as you speed down a tree-lined lane. A leaf catches in your front brake, causing the whirring sound you used to get with playing cards and clothespins. A falling leaf brushes your cheek as you ride through the forest on a breezy fall day.

—Dave Carter

A MOUNTAIN BIKE VACATION GUIDE

An excellent mountain bike vacation guide is America's Greatest Trails Guide, a special collector's edition published in summer 1992 by *Mountain Bike Action* magazine (see appendix). The guide features the best American destinations and trails, including a state-by-state directory of U.S. ski resort riding, as well as ideas for rides in Europe, Australia, and New Zealand.

For a copy, contact *Mountain Bike Action,* Hi-Torque Publications, 10600 Sepulveda Blvd., Mission Hills, CA 91345.

MOAB, UTAH

Located in eastern Utah, Moab is famous in mountain bike circles for its slickrock terrain and it attracts curious riders from around the world. Cyclists enjoy scenic and technical riding on smooth red rock amid an outstanding desert backdrop. Moab's trails are reported to be among the most challenging anywhere. Moab hosts its annual Fat Tire Festival each October, the week before Halloween. Canyonlands and Arches national parks are nearby, as is the trailhead for the famous 100-mile (161-km) Kokopelli's Trail, a mountain bike route that follows ancient Indian trails. The area's best riding is in the spring and fall; summer can be too hot.

Sports File/Todd Powell

Slickrock Trail challenges bikers from all over the world.

CRESTED BUTTE, COLORADO

This old-fashioned Victorian ski town in the western part of the state is where Colorado mountain biking began. It is also home to the Mountain Bike Hall of Fame and Museum, a small but growing tribute to the sport. In early July each year, Crested Butte fills up with mountain bike enthusiasts for its annual Fat Tire Bike Week. Old mining roads and single-track trails lead from the town into the magnificent surrounding mountains. Challenging climbs and descents abound and numerous loops can be explored.

David Epperson

Taking a break at Crested Butte en route to Pefri Pass.

MAMMOTH MOUNTAIN, CALIFORNIA

Situated in the Sierra Nevada about 7 hours north of Los Angeles and 5 hours east of San Francisco, Mammoth is a world-renowned ski resort. In summer, it becomes one of mountain biking's premier destinations and it hosts a large mountain bike festival each year. A variety of riding is available on the ski mountain and throughout surrounding areas, including June Lake, Mono Lake, Convict Lake, and Devil's Postpile. Mammoth became one of the first major resorts to embrace mountain biking. It hosted the NORBA World Mountain Bike Championships from 1987 to 1989 (coauthor Don Davis won the veteran class—age 35-plus—cross-country world championship in 1987 and placed second in 1988).

OTHER U.S. DESTINATIONS

Fine mountain bike destinations across the U.S. are receiving attention through festivals, races, and instructional programs. Excellent trail systems are being expanded and made more accessible to all levels of cyclists.

In the east, Mt. Snow, Vermont, has led the ski resort movement into mountain biking. It has operated a mountain bike school for several years and offers a wide variety of easy to very technical roads and trails. In New Hampshire's White Mountains and all across New England, today's more active leaf-lookers are taking autumn foliage tours on a range of scenic mountain bike trails.

Sports File/Brooks Dodge

Some of New England's most scenic routes can be found in Maine's Acadia National Park.

Lake Minnewaska State Park in New York's Hudson River country features more than 100 miles (161 km) of shale-packed roads and trails that beckon mountain bikers. Located near the town of New Paltz, the area offers fine scenery around Lake Armstrong and great views across the Catskill Mountains.

This is a good destination for both beginning and experienced riders who want to enjoy a weekend adventure. It is a convenient getaway for riders from the bustling New York metropolis.

Nearby Allaire State Park near Longbranch, New Jersey, and Ringwood State Park near Paramus, New Jersey, offer single-track and fire road rides. Steep Rock Reserve near Washington Depot, Connecticut, is a picturesque area with an abundance of beginner and intermediate terrain.

Other growing mountain bike centers in the eastern and central parts of the United States include Jim Thorpe, Pennsylvania, a small town in the Pocono Mountains that hosts its annual Mountain Bike Weekend Off-Road Festival every June; Chequamegon, in upstate Wisconsin, host of the Midwest's largest off-road festival and the Chequamegon 40 off-road race, held each summer; and Slaty Fork, West Virginia, home of the West Virginia Fat Tire Festival, held each year in mid-June.

Durango, Colorado, is a true mountain bike town and home to several of mountain biking's top competitors. It has hosted national competitions, and it holds a mountain bike festival every July and the annual Iron Horse Bicycle Classic festival (off- and on-road biking) every Memorial Day weekend. Vail is another Rocky Mountain destination. It offers mountain bike access to untamed high country scenery through the famed 10th Mountain Division trail and hut system. Sun Valley and Ketchum, Idaho, are base areas for rides to the lakes, old mines, and hot springs in the Sawtooth National Recreation Area.

Marin County, California, the birthplace of mountain biking, has trails winding through Mt. Tamalpais and Pine Mountain and beyond to Point Reyes National Seashore, although many of Mt. Tam's trails have been closed because of conflicts with hikers and other users. The Bodega Bay area to the north also offers scenic seaside riding. There is fine riding throughout the Sierra Nevada mountains, including in the Lake Tahoe area. In Southern California, the Snow Summit resort at Big Bear Lake holds summer and fall mountain bike festivals, attracting riders from the Los Angeles metropolitan area 2 hours away.

Western Europe by Mountain Bike

Mountain biking is a made-in-America sport that has been warmly embraced in Europe. American racer Mike Kloser won the 1988 World Mountain Bike Championships at Crans Montana, Switzerland, and the 1988 World Cup Finals at Torbole, Italy. Kloser, a resident of Vail, Colorado, lived, trained, and raced in Europe for 2 years.

"In many of the European areas, you'll find an abundance of more difficult terrain," says Kloser. "You'll encounter private trails and lanes but most of the time you will be allowed to pass through. There are many pedestrian paths and trails that were not designed for mountain bikes but

European Destinations

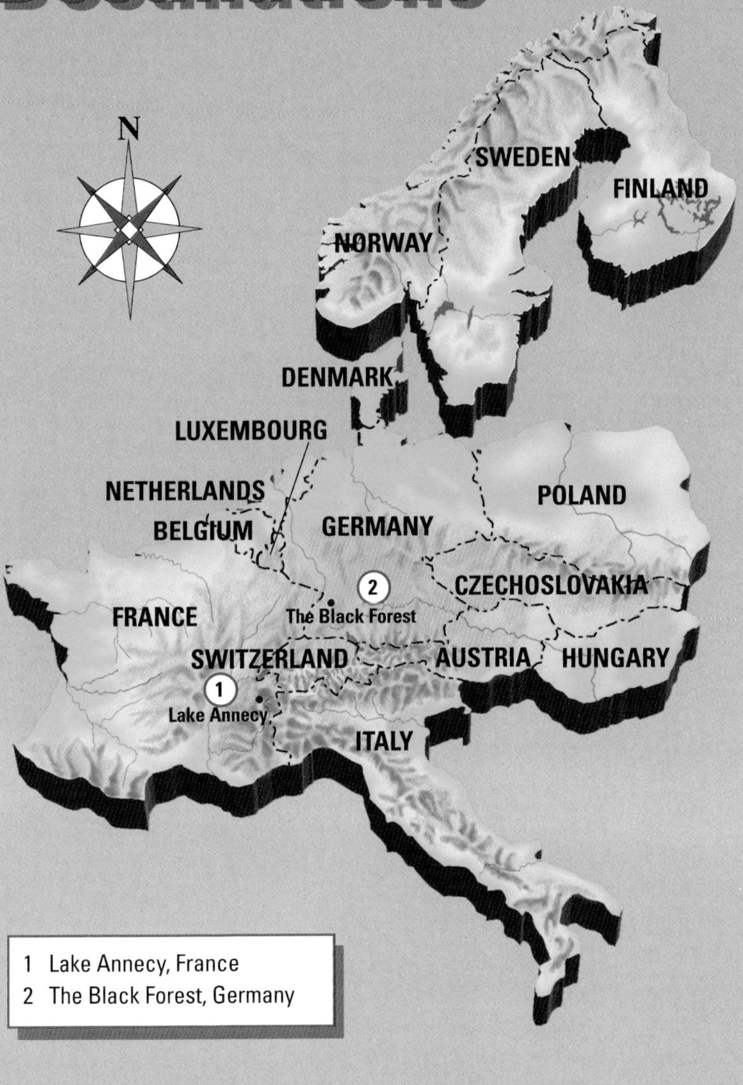

N

SWEDEN

FINLAND

NORWAY

DENMARK

LUXEMBOURG

NETHERLANDS

POLAND

BELGIUM

GERMANY

② The Black Forest

CZECHOSLOVAKIA

FRANCE

SWITZERLAND

AUSTRIA

HUNGARY

① Lake Annecy

ITALY

1 Lake Annecy, France
2 The Black Forest, Germany

if you demonstrate a polite attitude and cautious approach, you'll find there won't be too much conflict.''

Kloser lists these favorites:

ANZERE, SWITZERLAND

This area, located above the Valley of Sion and across from Crans Montana, offers an abundance of good trails and unpaved roads. Views of the snow-covered Matterhorn and Mt. Blanc can be seen from the hillside trails. There is a good mountain bike visitor program that offers guided rides, maps, and well-marked trails.

BIENNE, SWITZERLAND

Located near the northwest corner of Switzerland, this area is home to 1992 women's world champion, Sylvia Furst. The trails are diverse; many of the best rides are connected by sections of pavement. Great views overlook the lakes surrounding Bienne.

Switzerland is one big mountain biking opportunity.

LAKE ANNECY, FRANCE

Located about an hour west of Geneva and a half-hour north of the Olympic village of Albertville, this is a picturesque area in the foothills of the Alps. The hillsides around the lake are loaded with fun trails of all kinds, ranging from four-wheel-drive tracks to wooded and twisting single-tracks. The town offers a taste of the French lifestyle, and the lake has a variety of water sports.

David Epperson

The French Alps.

LAGO DIGARDA, ITALY

This is a summer tourist area situated in north-central Italy, just south of the Alps and Dolomites. Numerous trails circle the lake, with many heading off into the surrounding hills. Some use parts of old Roman roadways made of cobblestone. Plenty of local vineyards are found in the area.

THE BLACK FOREST, GERMANY

The Black Forest, near Baden Baden, is a favorite riding and training area for German cyclists. The wooded, rolling hills have many trails and old logging roads. Visitors should stop at the old Roman baths in the historic town of Baden Baden (which translates to bath bath).

MORE EUROPEAN FAVORITES

Other riders have reported fine riding opportunities throughout the mountainous regions of France, Spain, Germany, Austria, and Switzerland. Some of the world's most scenic mountain terrain is found in the Alpine countries of Europe.

Good riding has been reported in the Pyrenees along the Spanish–French border, in the small towns of the Bavarian Alps, such as Garmisch and Berchtesgaden, and in many resort communities in the Austrian Alps. Good reports have come from riders visiting the Bernese Oberland of Switzerland including Interlaken, Grindelwald, Wengen, and Murren. The famed peaks Eiger and Jungfrau are in this region. The Davos-Klosters area has hosted World Cup racing.

David Epperson

Biking in Tuscany, Italy, affords glimpses of picturesque villas.

Franklin Henry, a Colorado-based pro racer who has ridden in many countries, suggests riding in the southern reaches of the Black Forest, near Freiburg, Germany, where long asphalt bike trails lead to a wide network of off-road trails, including flat and mountainous terrain. Scenery includes farms, trains, castle ruins, and old battlefields. Local bike shops have maps that show trails as well as historical attractions.

Henry also likes the Strasbourg area just north in the Rhine River valley, which features excellent riding through rolling valleys and vineyards. He also suggests the hills above Munich, where nice terrain and guided tours are available.

In southeastern Belgium, Henry recommends the Ardennes area, which includes Hoffalize, a World Cup race site. The area features hilly to mountainous terrain with rich forests and abundant single-track trails.

Bike Britain

Well-known British cyclist Simon Burney, author of a book on mountain bike racing and manager of a mountain bike race team, is enthusiastic about the riding opportunities in Great Britain. He recommends national parks in the mountainous areas, where the trails are challenging and the scenery is attractive.

Burney cautions that off-road riding is allowed only on public bridleways and that in some sensitive areas, even the bridleways are closed. The British Mountain Bike Federation has developed links with other outdoor groups and is working to expand mountain bike access.

"Don't be put off by the wet weather attributed to the British Isles," Burney says. "The island climate means constant changes. Wet weather seldom stays long. A rainy day can turn sunny in a few hours."

First National Park in the Peak District of Derbyshire is located at the south end of the Pennine Chain (the Backbone of Britain). Popular with tourists, and a training ground for most British professional cyclists, it features a variety of riding terrain at Moorlands and Rocky Edges.

The Lake District is one of Britain's most popular mountain areas. England's highest mountains are found here, topped by Scafell Pikes. Stunning scenery and lakes abound.

Scotland offers Britain's highest mountains, including Ben Nevis. The Aviemore ski area is popular among mountain bikers, having hosted World Cup races 1988 through 1991.

Stockfile/Steven Behr

The white cliffs of Dover offer a scenic ride in southern England.

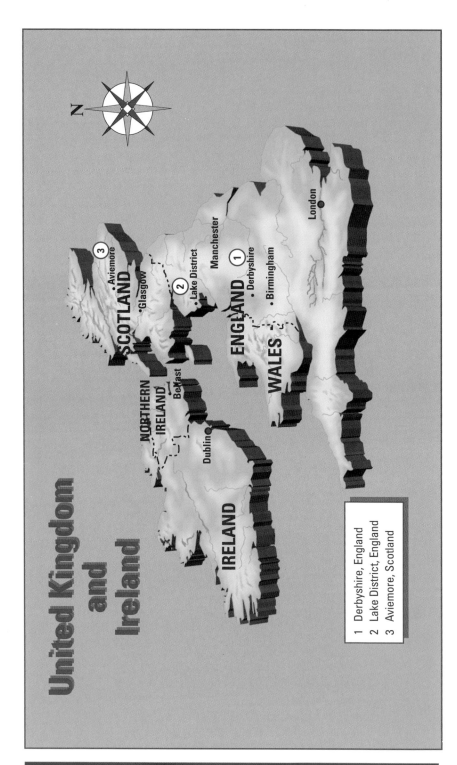

United Kingdom and Ireland

1 Derbyshire, England
2 Lake District, England
3 Aviemore, Scotland

Canada's Trails

In Canada, mountain bikers have discovered fine trails in the Whistler-Blackcomb resort areas of British Columbia. Franklin Henry is partial to the town of Squamish just north of Vancouver and its beautiful trails along the Strait of Georgia.

Mountain bikers also are taking in the grandeur of the Canadian Rockies resort areas near Banff. To the east, the Bromont resort in Quebec has hosted world-class competitions.

THE WEST

Highlands in Victoria, British Columbia, features an extensive maze of fire roads and trails for exploration by all levels of mountain bikers. Another favorite, near Lake Mathison Park, is the Galloping Goose Trail, a scenic route that follows 80 kilometers (50 miles) of old railroad trail.

On the highway between Banff and Jasper in Alberta.

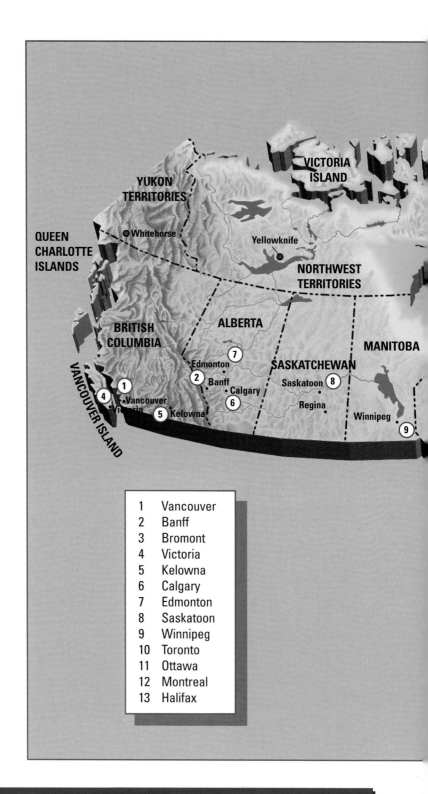

1 Vancouver
2 Banff
3 Bromont
4 Victoria
5 Kelowna
6 Calgary
7 Edmonton
8 Saskatoon
9 Winnipeg
10 Toronto
11 Ottawa
12 Montreal
13 Halifax

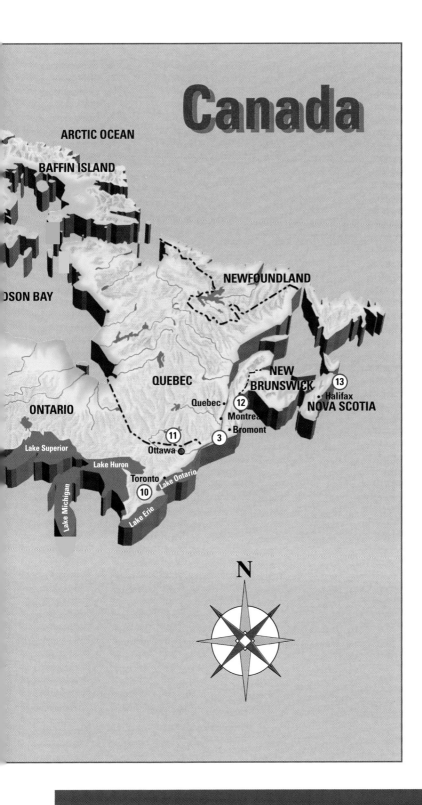

Canada

ARCTIC OCEAN

BAFFIN ISLAND

HUDSON BAY

NEWFOUNDLAND

QUEBEC

ONTARIO

Lake Superior

Lake Huron

Lake Michigan

Lake Erie

Lake Ontario

Quebec

Montreal

Bromont

Ottawa

Toronto

NEW BRUNSWICK

NOVA SCOTIA

Halifax

⑬

⑫

③

⑪

⑩

N

Paul Morrison

The Vancouver skyline provides a beautiful backdrop for this ride.

The Mt. Seymour Ski Area in Vancouver, BC, is noted for its steep terrain with advanced and technical riding. Some trails are moderately difficult. Grouse Mountain and Cypress Mountain are also ski areas that offer difficult riding.

Kettle Valley, located in Kelowna in BC's interior, offers a desert type terrain with riding along abandoned railway alignments. The terrain is rated as beginner to intermediate. Penticton's Apex Mountain, also in BC, is a ski area featuring fire roads and forested trails.

The Bragg Creek and Kananaskis East trails are popular with Calgary, Alberta, mountain bikers. Small cross-country ski areas at White Mud Creek and River Valley Trails in Edmonton, Alberta, offer single-track and double-track riding along streams and rivers.

In Saskatoon, Saskatchewan, Meewasin Valley Trails offers rolling cross-country terrain rated good for beginning riders.

Rose Isle in Winnipeg, Manitoba, is a cross-country ski area with miles of single-track and double-track trails through rolling hills and deciduous forests. This is also a great area for beginners.

THE SHIELD
Seaton Trail, located near Toronto, Ontario, is a well-groomed path suitable for beginners. Hockey Valley features easy to intermediate cross-country and fire trails through aspen groves. Orangeville Trails is a cross-country ski trail system offering great beginner and intermediate

riding through gentle, rolling terrain. Gatineau Parc, close to Ottawa, Ontario, offers well-groomed trails and terrain suitable for first-time mountain bikers.

Parc De Paul Sauve, Le Calvaier Trails, and Mt. Tremblant all offer mountain biking on varied terrain near Montreal, Quebec, including hiking trails, cross-country ski trails, and fire roads. Mt. Tremblant offers the most challenging rides with terrain rated moderate to very technical. It also offers fine autumn scenery.

THE ATLANTIC
Jimmy's Roundtop offers challenging riding over scenic, rolling, and rocky single-track and double-track trails in Halifax, Nova Scotia. Another local favorite is Old St. Margret's Bay Road, with scenic, rocky terrain.

Scenic Australia and New Zealand

Mountain biking is also catching on down under. Enterprising mountain bike tour operators are billing trips to the Great Barrier Reef region and the endless white beaches of Queensland. Australian and foreign riders can take rides and organized tours through the outback and through mountainous jungles that feature rain forests and exotic plants.

Australia has a mountain bike race circuit with stops at cities including Sydney, Melbourne, and Cairns. The Thredbo ski area near Sydney has hosted international-level mountain bike competition.

Fine riding is reported in Australia's Snowy Mountains, which are also known as the Australian Alps. A popular area is the Kosciusko National Park, which offers challenging riding on numerous fire trails.

In New Zealand, Auckland native Stephen Swart is one of the top competitive road cyclists. He is a former Tour of New Zealand winner and third-place finisher in the 1992 Tour DuPont.

Swart recommends many areas here but cautions that mountain biking is still relatively new. ''Be sure to check with local agencies for rules governing mountain biking in all of these areas, and be sure to obey private property signs,'' he says.

The Coromandel Peninsula, in the northeast section of North Island, across from Auckland, offers miles of roads and single-track trails. Swart suggests ending a ride at Hot Water Beach by enjoying a dip in the natural hot springs. The town of Rotorua, in the center of North Island, is at the hub of many great trails. There are forested logging roads around Lake Taupo and the Bay of Plenty. To the north, the Tangariro National Forest

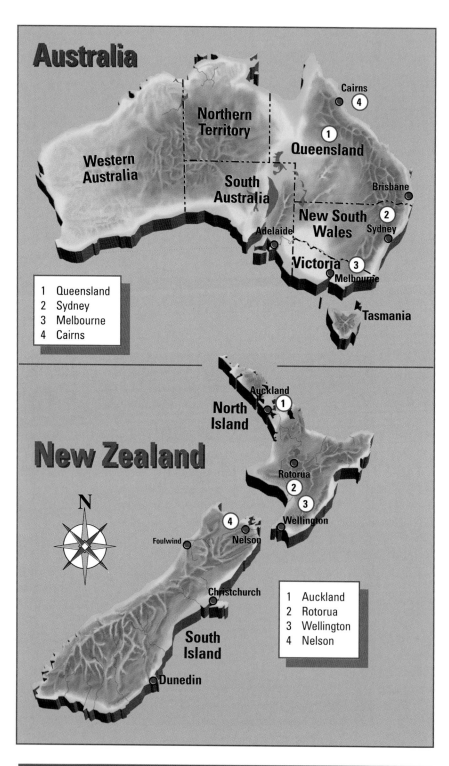

Australia

Northern Territory

Western Australia

South Australia

Queensland

New South Wales

Victoria

Tasmania

Cairns (4)

(1)

Brisbane

(2) Sydney

Adelaide

(3)

Melbourne

1	Queensland
2	Sydney
3	Melbourne
4	Cairns

New Zealand

N

North Island

South Island

Auckland (1)

Rotorua (2)

(3) Wellington

(4) Nelson

Foulwind

Christchurch

Dunedin

1	Auckland
2	Rotorua
3	Wellington
4	Nelson

Lake Rotoetti in New Zealand—a scene of peaceful reflection.

offers spectacular riding around three volcanos. The Wellington area, at the southern end of North Island, offers riding on roads and trails in the hills surrounding coastal resorts.

Nelson, at the north end of South Island, is at the base of a mountainous area, and many of its trails climb into the higher elevations. Lake Tekapo borders the Southern Alps in the central part of South Island and offers many possibilities for exploring around small lakes. Finally, Swart suggests the area north of Marlborough Sound, on South Island, for riding through forests overlooking scenic bays.

6

PURSUING MOUNTAIN BIKING FURTHER

Now that you're familiar with the basics of mountain biking, it's time for some ideas for riders who want to get into the competitive side of the sport.

It is beyond the scope of this book to cover details of serious training and competition; there are specialized books on the market dealing with those matters (see the appendix). The purpose here is to provide an introductory look into racing and other competitions.

Racing

This is a great way to test yourself and your abilities. Don't worry that you haven't raced before; most mountain bike competitions have categories for first-timers as well as for age and skill level. In the U.S., most races sanctioned by the National Off-Road Bicycle Association (NORBA) will issue one-day race licenses to beginning racers. Many riders enter races just for fun and to measure their own abilities by charting their development as riders. Race against yourself, not against the pack.

Competition categories in most mountain bike races include Beginner, for the first-time competitor; Sport, for the intermediate competitor; Expert, for the advanced competitor; and Pro/Elite, status granted on request.

Age classes are Junior, ages 12-18; Senior, ages 19-34; Veteran, ages 35-44; and Master, age 45 and older.

Just another day at the races.

TYPES OF RACES

There are several different types of mountain bike competitions, ranging from endurance events such as cross-country races to exciting, fast-paced action such as the downhill. If any of these events seems exciting to you, pursue it!

Cross-country—A mass start event contested on dirt roads and trails, and sometimes on a limited amount of pavement. Cross-country races are usually held on circuits of 2 miles (3.2 km) or longer.

Point-to-point—A mass start event starting at one point and ending at another. Terrain is similar to a cross-country race.

Hill climb—A timed event with either individual or mass starts. As the name indicates, the course climbs to a finish at a higher elevation than the start. Hill climbs can range from moderate to some of the toughest endurance tests in the world.

Downhill—An exciting event for riders and spectators, the downhill is the most dangerous of mountain bike races. It is usually an individual time trial with starts at specific intervals, such as 30 seconds or 1 minute. Each racer is timed from the start to a lower elevation finish line.

Dual slalom—Riders compete next to one another on side-by-side courses in a format similar to dual slalom ski racing. The rider must go through each gate on his or her own course. Riders switch courses for a second run. The best combined time from two runs wins. Penalties are assessed for false starts, crashing, or missing a gate.

Stage race—A stage race might typically include a cross-country, uphill, and downhill. Winners of each event are recognized with points, and the rider with the total point lead or lowest combined time is the overall winner. This event is a good measurement of all-around skills.

Ultraendurance—Mountain biking's answer to the marathon. Ultraendurance races are more than 75 miles (121 km) long.

Observed Trials

Trials competitions are one of mountain biking's most interesting spectator events. Held in a compact, arena-like setting, trials events often attract large crowds. In trials, riders must negotiate a series of challenging obstacle courses. Obstacles may include logs, large rocks, giant boulders, water, mud, a combination of these, and severely uneven terrain.

Most trials events have stock and modified bicycle classes. Riders compete on regular mountain bikes in the stock class; serious trials riders compete in the modified bike class using small, specially designed trials bikes with 20-inch wheels.

Just one of many obstacles in the trials at Mt. Snow, Vermont.

The trials competitor attempts to ride over or through each obstacle, staying within set boundaries and not putting a foot on the ground. Putting a foot down is called a dab. When a rider completes a section without dabbing or going out of bounds he is said to have ''cleaned'' the section.

Trials are scored on points, with the lowest total winning. Each dab is a point against you. Five points is the worst you can score in one section.

Most trials events have 5 to 10 sections in which the rider is judged and scored. There are individual and combined winners.

Stunts

Mountain bike stunts are best learned from more experienced riders. Go to a trials event and you will see stunts you would never have imagined. Talk to the competitors; most will be happy to give you a few pointers on how to practice.

Many advanced trials maneuvers are more difficult than they may appear when performed by an expert rider so be careful in your attempts.

For example, if you want to learn to jump obstacles, start with small, forgiving objects. Jump over a styrofoam cup and practice until you are

Difficult stunts like this require expert skill.

perfect every time before you try progressively higher jumps like a curb, log, or park bench.

These stunts can take as much or more time to master than training for a cross-country mountain bike race. Stunts can be fun but be prepared to take some tumbles if this is your kind of thrill.

Mountain Bike Polo

This is a hot social sport that is gaining popularity with mountain bikers around the globe. The only specialized equipment needed are mallets and balls which may be obtained through the World Bicycle Polo Federation (see the appendix) or a dealer near you.

Mountain bike polo is played on a flat field, 160 feet (48.8 m) long by 90 feet (27.4 m) wide, with 12-foot (3.7-m) wide goals at each end. A match consists of two 10-minute time periods called chukkers.

"It's not an endurance sport. It's more strategy than stamina," says Zachi Anderson, owner of a bicycle shop in Grass Valley, California, and a member of the 1989 California state champion bicycle polo team.

The official rule book calls for four-person coed teams. The ball may be played only parallel to the sidelines to avoid dangerous collisions. Anderson says a typical strategy is a rotating play where riders ride through the goal zone and then circle back down the sideline and back onto the field of play.

According to Anderson, a typical match might include 10 or 12 goals, although good defensive teams can often hold the opposition scoreless.

John Laptad/F-Stock

A new way to compete on a bike—playing polo.

Moab, Utah, hosts a World Bicycle Polo Championship each October as part of its annual Fat Tire Festival. The event has attracted teams from across the United States.

Training

Consistency is the key to successful training for any mountain bike competition. Work on increasing your workouts in both length and intensity. Develop and follow a cycling program and consider cross-training. This will improve your cycling and help avoid burnout from overtraining. Weight lifting will increase your strength, and running will help you aerobically. Cross-country and downhill skiing, ice skating, and in-line skating work many of the same muscles as cycling and are cross-training methods used by competitive mountain bikers.

Make It Fun

Enter a competitive event with some of your cycling pals. Don't worry about winning; pace each other and measure your abilities against the best racers or trials competitors in the field. Enter the proper class as a beginner and you will improve rapidly. To be successful, you need to master the basics. Work on fitness and practice technique and maneuvers in a variety of terrains.

This kind of intense competition requires a consistent training regimen.

Mountain biking at advanced levels requires time and practice. Focus your efforts on climbing, descending, cornering, shifting, braking, and riding over obstacles smoothly and efficiently. As you ride, read the terrain. Braking, shifting, and balancing through the technical sections will become second nature. Your level of skill will develop in time. Be patient; learn to control your speed and if a section of trail is too difficult, get off and walk or carry your bike. Go back later and ride the tough, technical sections. Don't be too quick to judge yourself against the racers.

Riding with others is the key to riding faster and farther. The best way to develop greater proficiency is to take on new terrain with others who are at or slightly above your skill level. If your companion is a much better rider, you will suffer at his or her pace. Plus, your safety could be at stake.

If there is a mountain bike club or race group in your area, join in on a ride. You will quickly identify your strengths and weaknesses. Are you a strong climber? A downhill daredevil? Get together with some friends for some mountain bike polo, a true test of bike handling skills. Or test yourself at a trials event. Go to a race as a spectator and watch the pros tackle the toughest obstacle or course. Visualize yourself in their position.

SAFETY TIP Before a competition, or any ride for that matter, check your brakes, brake-pad–wheel alignment, tire pressure, cable tensions, and gears. Pay attention to your gear adjustments; a mountain bike event will almost always demand that your low range gears work perfectly.

Make sure your stem bolt and handlebars are tight; steering can be stressed during tough race conditions. Finally, check the quick releases on your wheels and make sure they are firmly in place, but not overtightened.

If you are not confident in making these adjustments on your own, check with your bike shop for advice.

SAMPLE RACE TRAINING PROGRAM

Here's a basic training program to use as a guideline:

Monday: 1 to 2 hours of steady pedaling on easy terrain at a cadence of 90 to 110 revolutions per minute. Easy spinning, no big gears. If you use a heart rate monitor or measure your pulse manually, use a target 10 or 20 beats below your maximum heart rate (remember, 220 minus your age equals maximum heart rate). For best results, most of your training should be in the 60 percent to 85 percent range of maximum.

Tuesday: 1 hour to 90 minutes of off-road riding with average heart rate in the 60 percent to 85 percent range.

Wednesday: 1 to 2 hours of riding at 70 percent to 85 percent of maximum. This should simulate race pace and duration.

Thursday: Intensity near maximum. Warm up for a half-hour, then begin intervals. These are 45- to 60-second bursts at near maximum effort. Progress to six or eight efforts, with adequate recovery time between. For maximum effect, intervals can be increased to 2 to 3 minutes each. Be sure your heart rate returns below the threshold level before doing the next interval. These intervals will simulate the first mile or so of a mountain bike race, allowing you to make this kind of effort and then recover for optimum performance throughout the race.

Friday: Rest.

Saturday: 1 hour to 90 minutes of easy riding at 60 percent of your maximum heart rate.

Sunday: Race day. Good luck!

If you are limited by time, which we all are, try to train for at least 40 to 60 minutes per day at or near your training threshold. It is generally agreed that 20 minutes at this level will generate a training effect.

Make your training fun and not too regimented. Alternate your easy and hard days. Remember, it is best to be well rested coming into a race.

Your overall fitness is best maintained with some activity every day (20 to 40 minutes) that will increase your heart rate. Fitness needs to be part of daily life, especially as we get older.

APPENDIX

FOR MORE INFORMATION

Cycling Organizations

Bicycle Federation of Australia, Inc.
P.O. Box 869
Artarmon, NSW 2064 Australia
(02) 412-1041

Bicycle Institute of America (BIA)
1818 R St., NW
Washington, DC 20009 USA
(202) 332-6986/fax (202) 332-6989

Bikecentennial
P.O. Box 8308
Missoula, MT 59807 USA
(406) 721-1776

British Mountain Bike Federation
36 Rockingham Rd.
Kettering, Northampton, England
(44) 536-412211/fax (44) 536-412142

Canadian Cycling Association (CCA)
1600 James Naismith
Gloucester, ON, Canada K1B 5N4

International Mountain Bicycling Association (IMBA)
P.O. Box 412043
Los Angeles, CA 90041 USA
(818) 792-8830/fax (818) 796-2299

League of American Wheelmen (LAW)
190 West Ostend St., Suite 120
Baltimore, MD 21230 USA
(410) 539-3399

Mountain Bike Hall of Fame and Museum
P.O. Box 845
Crested Butte, CO 81224 USA
(303) 349-7382

National Off-Road Bicycle Association (NORBA)
1750 East Boulder St.
Colorado Springs, CO 80909 USA
(719) 578-4717/fax (719) 578-4596

United States Bicycling Hall of Fame
34 East Main St.
Somerville, NJ 08876 USA
(800) BICYCLE or (201) 722-3620

United States Cycling Federation (USCF)
1750 East Boulder St.
Colorado Springs, CO 80909 USA
(719) 578-4581

Women's Mountain Biking and Tea Society (WOMBATS)
P.O. Box 757
Fairfax, CA 94930 USA

World Bicycle Polo Federation
P.O. Box 1039
Bailey, CO 80421 USA
(303) 838-7431

Books

All-Terrain Biking: Skills and Techniques for Mountain Bikers
Jim Zarka
Bicycle Books
P.O. Box 2038
Mill Valley, CA 94941 USA
$7.95

Bicycle Mechanics
Steve Snowling and Ken Evans
Human Kinetics
Box 5076
Champaign, IL 61825-5076 USA
$18.95

Bicycle Technology
Rob van der Plas
Bicycle Books
P.O. Box 2038
Mill Valley, CA 94941 USA
$16.95

Cuthbertson's Little Mountain Bike Book
Tom Cuthbertson
Ten Speed Press
P.O. Box 7123
Berkeley, CA 94707 USA
$5.95

Mountain Bike! A Manual of Beginning to Advanced Technique
William Nealy
Menasha Ridge Press
3169 Cahaba Heights Rd.
Birmingham, AL 35243 USA
$12.95

Mountain Bike Handbook
Rob van der Plas
Sterling
387 Park Ave. S
New York, NY 10016 USA
$10.95

Mountain Bike Magic
Rob van der Plas
Bicycle Books
P.O. Box 2038
Mill Valley, CA 94941 USA
$14.95

Mountain Bike Racing
Tim Gould and Simon Burney
Springfield Books
Norman Rd., Denby Dale
Huddersfield, HD88TH
West Yorkshire, England
$22.50

The Mountain Bike Repair Handbook
Dennis Coello
Lyons and Burford
31 W. 21st St.
New York, NY 10010 USA
$12.95

Mountain Bike Techniques
Dennis Coello
Lyons and Burford
31 W. 21st St.
New York, NY 10010 USA
$7.95

Mountain Bikes: Maintenance and Repair
John Stevenson
Bicycle Books
P.O. Box 2038
Mill Valley, CA 94941 USA
$22.50

Mountain Biking for Mere Mortals
Michael Hodgson
ICS Books
One Tower Plaza
107 E. 89th Ave.
Merrillville, IN 46410 USA
$6.99

Science of Cycling
Edmund R. Burke
Human Kinetics
Box 5076
Champaign, IL 61825-5076 USA
$15.95

Periodicals

Australian Cyclist
P.O. Box 869
Artarmon, NSW 2064 Australia
(02) 412-1041

Bicycle Guide
545 Boylston St.
Boston, MA 02116 USA
(617) 236-1885/fax (617) 267-1849

Bicycling & Mountain Bike
33 E. Minor St.
Emmaus, PA 18098 USA
(215) 967-5171/fax (215) 967-8960

Bikereport
Bikecentennial
P.O. Box 8308
Missoula, MT 59807 USA
(406) 721-1776

Cycling USA
United States Cycling Federation
1750 E. Boulder St.
Colorado Springs, CO 80909 USA
(719) 578-4581

Dirt Rag
AKA Productions
460 Maple Ave.
Springdale, PA 15144 USA
(412) 274-4529

IMBA Trail News
International Mountain Bicycling Association
P.O. Box 1212
Crested Butte, CO 81224 USA
(303) 349-7104

Mountain and City Biking
7950 Deering Ave.
Canoga Park, CA 91304 USA
(818) 887-0550

Mountain Bike Action
Hi-Torque Publications
10600 Sepulveda Blvd.
Mission Hills, CA 91345 USA
(818) 365-6831

NORBA News
National Off-Road Bicycle Association
1750 E. Boulder St.
Colorado Springs, CO 80909 USA
(719) 578-4717/fax (719) 578-4596

Pedal
Canadian Cycling News
2 Pardee Ave., Suite 204
Toronto, ON, Canada M6K 3H5
(416) 530-1350/fax (416) 530-4155

Competition Periodicals

Velo News
1830 N. 55th St.
Boulder, CO 80301 USA
(303) 440-0601

Winning
744 Roble Rd., Suite 190
Allentown, PA 18103 USA
(215) 266-6893

Bicycle Trade Magazines

American Bicyclist
Cycling Press
80 Eighth Ave.
New York, NY 10011 USA
(212) 206-7230/fax (212) 633-0079

Bicycle Business Journal
P.O. Box 1570
Fort Worth, TX 76101 USA
(817) 870-0341/fax (817) 332-1619

Bicycle Retailer & Industry News
1444-C S. St. Francis Dr.
Santa Fe, NM 87501 USA
(505) 988-5099/fax (505) 988-7224

Bicycle Today
Bicycle Today Magazine Co.
5, Lane, 226, Sung Chiang Rd.
Taipei, Taiwan, ROC
(02) 5718626

Mail Order Catalogs

Bike Nashbar
4111 Simon Rd.
Youngstown, OH 44512-1343 USA
(216) 782-2244

California Bicycle Supply
P.O. Box 470502
San Francisco, CA 94123 USA
(415) 349-9539 or (800) 999-4745

Campmor
P.O. Box 998
Paramus, NJ 07653 USA
(201) 445-5000

The Colorado Cyclist
3970 E. Bijou St.
Colorado Springs, CO 80909-9946 USA
(719) 591-4040 or (800) 688-8600

Excel Sports International
3275 Prairie Ave., Suite 1
Boulder, CO 80301 USA
(303) 444-6737 or (800) 627-6664

LL Bean, Inc.
LL Street
Freeport, ME 04033 USA
(800) 221-4221

Performance Bicycle
P.O. Box 2741
Chapel Hill, NC 27515-2741 USA
(800) 727-2433

Tours and Travel

Backroads Bicycle Touring (worldwide)
1516 Fifth St.
Berkeley, CA 94710-1740 USA
(510) 527-1555
(800) 245-3874

Cycle America (U.S.)
P.O. Box 29B
Northfield, MN 55057 USA
(800) 245-3263

Outer Edge Expeditions (heli-lift mountain biking, New Zealand)
45500 Pontiac Trail
Walled Lake, MI 48390 USA
(313) 624-5140 or (800) 322-5235

Tailwinds Bicycle Tours (Australia)
72 Wattle St.
Lyneham, ACT 2602 Australia
(06) 249-6122

Timberline Bicycle Tours (Rocky Mountains, Pacific states)
7975 E. Harvard, #J
Denver, CO 80231 USA
(303) 759-3804

VCC Four Seasons Cycling (U.S. East Coast, eastern Canada)
P.O. Box 145
Waterbury Center, VT 05677 USA
(802) 244-5135

Western Spirit Cycling (Rocky Mountains)
P.O. Box 411
Moab, UT 84532 USA
(801) 259-8732 or (800) 845-BIKE

MOUNTAIN BIKING LINGO

access—Term used to describe riding areas available to mountain bikers, as in public land access.

aerobic exercise—Muscular activity that is fueled by oxygen.

anaerobic exercise—Muscular activity at an intense rate, not fueled by oxygen. Such exercise can be maintained for only a short time; oxygen is eventually required to enable recovery.

bonk—To run out of energy.

braze-on fitting—A piece soldered to the frame (usually with silver or brass) for attaching such extras as water bottle cages and cable guide eyelets.

bunny hop—A maneuver to jump obstacles such as logs, rocks, or curbs in which both wheels leave the ground. In a wheelie hop, only the front tire leaves the ground.

cantilever brakes—Style of brakes most common to the mountain bike and hybrid bike. Attached by two bosses that are brazed on the front and rear fork stays.

chain breaker—Tool for pushing pin in or out to attach or remove chain. Also called a chain tool.

cleaning a section—Riding over an area without putting a foot down.

clunker—An old-fashioned 26-inch single-speed bike, or the very earliest design of mountain bike.

crank—Arm that attaches the pedal to the bottom-bracket spindle.

cyclo-cross bike—Bike similar to a road bike, with turned-down handlebar, cantilever brakes, and narrow tires. Used for cyclo-cross training and racing on part-dirt, part-pavement courses.

derailleur—Mechanism in front and rear that moves the chain between gears.

downshift—To shift to a lower, or easier, gear.

endo—A dramatic over-the-handlebar crash. See *face-plant*.

etiquette—Showing good judgment in trail use and respecting other users.

face-plant—A nasty wreck in which the rider eats dirt. May or may not be an endo.

fall line—The most direct route down a hill.

fat tire—The kind of tire used on a mountain bike. Also a term used to describe mountain bike–related things, as in fat tire festival.

fire road—Single lane, one-vehicle-width roads in the hills that serve as fire breaks and allow emergency vehicle access.

gonzo—Crazy; somewhat weird.

granny gear—Small chainring, used mainly for climbing.

hub—Center of wheel; point at which spokes attach.

index shifting—Sometimes referred to as click shifting. Changing one gear up or down for each click stop in the particular derailleur system used.

kamikaze—A daredevil mountain biker.

panniers—Luggage carriers for touring.

quick release—Lever mechanism for easy removal and attachment of wheels or seat.

single-track—Narrow trail on which cyclists must ride in single file. A double-track trail allows two bikes side by side.

slickrock—Smooth rock hills that offer challenging riding (a Utah specialty).

stem—The piece that attaches the handlebar to the frame.

step-in pedal—Enables stable attachment between cleated shoe and pedal. A sideward twist will usually release the connection. Also known as clipless pedal.

suspension—Design feature that provides shock absorption. Front suspension can be through suspension forks or stem. Rear suspension can use a pivoting rear triangle or suspended seat lever. *Fully suspended* is a term used to describe a bike with front and rear suspension.

switchback—A 90-degree or greater turn on a road or trail.

toe clip—Pedal attachment that helps hold the foot on the pedal. Usually combined with a toe strap.

topo map—A localized topographical map showing elevations and other geographic features.

U-brake—Style of brake. Used as a rear brake on some bikes.

upshift—To shift into a higher, or harder, gear.

INDEX

ABOUT THE AUTHORS

Don Davis   **Dave Carter**

Don Davis is a sponsorship coordinator for Bell Sports, Inc. He is also an expert on mountain biking, having been involved in the activity since the late 1970s when it was just beginning to develop. In addition to recreational riding, Don has spent more than a decade racing mountain bikes on the professional and veteran mountain biking circuits. In 1987 he finished first in the Veteran Mountain Bike Cross Country World Championships, and in 1988 he finished second.

Before getting involved in mountain biking, Don competed both nationally and internationally in road bicycling for over 20 years. He was the 1968 California State Junior Road Champion.

Don received his bachelor's degree in health science from San Jose State University in 1973. He is a member of both the National Off-Road Bicycle Association and the United States Cycling Federation. Don now lives in Campbell, CA, where in his free time he enjoys skiing, tennis, swimming, and hiking.

Dave Carter is a freelance writer and a community relations specialist who resides in Nevada City, CA. As a longtime skier and former ski patrolman, he took up mountain biking as a way to stay in shape for ski season. He became hooked and now rides year-round.

Dave has an extensive writing background including 12 years experience as a writer and correspondent for major daily newspapers. He also has had numerous articles published in leading travel, outdoor, and sports magazines. Whenever he gets the chance, Dave combines his job as a writer with his love for biking. He not only has worked as a publicist for the West Coast's first mountain bike park at the Eagle Mountain ski area, but also has helped promote and publicize the Tour of Nevada City Bicycle Classic.

Dave received his bachelor's degree in mass communications from California State University at Fullerton in 1973. His leisure activities include skiing, softball, and cycling.

Photo Credits

Pages 4, 5 (top), 6 (top): Special thanks to TREK USA
9, 26-27, 31, 47: Courtesy of Bell Sports
17: Rich Cruse/courtesy of Bell Sports
18: Malcolm Fearon/Singletrack Photography
32, 53, 54: Mark Thayer/courtesy of Bell Sports
22, 35, 67-69, 72-74: Wilmer Zehr/special thanks to Champaign Cycle Co.
37, 76, 112, 114, 117: Tom Moran/Singletrack Photography
56, 82: Beth Schneider
65, 88: Bob Winsett/TOM STACK & ASSOCIATES
83: Neal A. Palumbo/Singletrack Photography
98: Spencer Swanger/TOM STACK & ASSOCIATES
103, 109: Markham Johnson/Backroads Bicycle Touring
106: Paul Morrison, Box 162, Whistler, British Columbia, Canada V0N 1B0
115: Alan Hardy/courtesy of Bell Sports